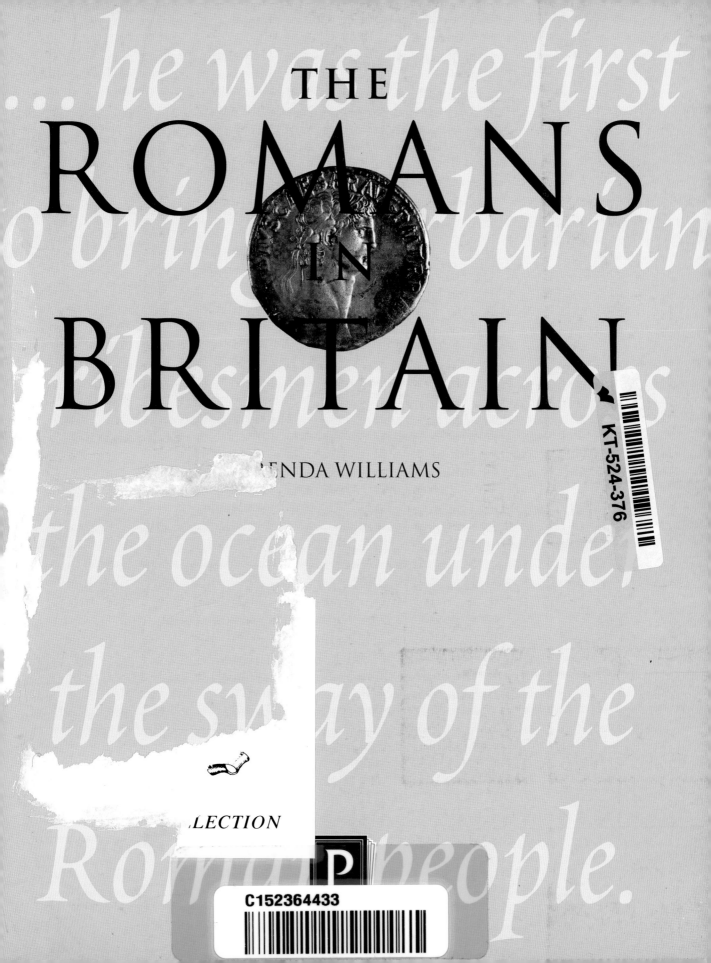

THE ROMANS IN BRITAIN

BRENDA WILLIAMS

...he was the first
o bring barbarian
the ocean under
the sway of the
Roman people.

Publication in this form copyright © Jarrold Publishing 2004.

Text copyright © Jarrold Publishing.

The moral right of the author has been asserted.

Series editor Angela Royston.

Edited by Clare Collinson.

Designed by Nick Avery.

Picture research by Jan Kean.

The family tree on page 7 was prepared by Nick Avery.

The artwork on pages 68–9 and 84–5 was created by Roger Hutchins.

Maps by The Map Studio, Romsey, Hampshire. The map on the ifc flap and page 19 is based on a map created by John Buckley.

A CIP catalogue for this book is available from the British Library.

Published by:
Jarrold Publishing
Healey House, Dene Road, Andover, Hampshire, SP10 2AA
www.britguides.com

Set in Minion.
Printed in Singapore.

ISBN 1 84165 127 3   1/04

Pitkin is an imprint of Jarrold Publishing, Norwich.

CONTENTS

BRITAIN JOINS THE ROMAN WORLD   4

BRITAIN'S 'BARBARIANS'   6

BRITAIN BECOMES BRITANNIA   18

SETTLING IN   36

ROMANIZING BRITAIN   52

CIVILIZED LIFE   60

THE ROMANS DEPART   88

INDEX   95

BRITAIN JOINS THE ROMAN WORLD

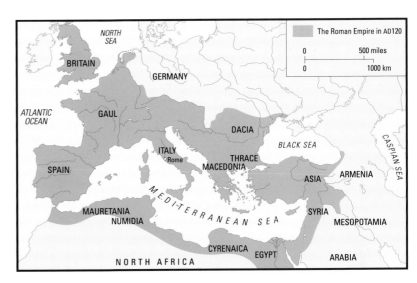

The Roman Empire in AD120

NORTH SEA · BRITAIN · GERMANY · ATLANTIC OCEAN · GAUL · DACIA · ITALY · Rome · THRACE · MACEDONIA · BLACK SEA · SPAIN · CASPIAN SEA · ASIA · ARMENIA · MAURETANIA · NUMIDIA · MEDITERRANEAN SEA · SYRIA · MESOPOTAMIA · CYRENAICA · EGYPT · ARABIA · NORTH AFRICA

JULIUS CAESAR TOLD EVERYBODY that he came, saw and conquered. He made Gaul (today's France, Belgium and Germany west of the Rhine) part of the Roman Empire and its Celtic people into 'new Romans'. Caesar also came and saw Britain, but never actually conquered it. To the Romans the island seemed remote and foggy, though rich in minerals and fertile farmland, peopled by quarrelling tribes who painted themselves blue, drove chariots, drank beer and had no writing. Could such a land become part of the Roman civilized world?

In AD 43, almost 100 years after Caesar's expeditions, Romans returned to conquer Britain, or at least the southern part of it. British Celts, descended from earlier migrant settlers, were about to be 'Romanized'. United to some degree by language and culture, the Celtic tribes were fractious politically, and unable to match the disciplined savagery of the Roman legions.

The invasion of AD 43 introduced Britain into history. In came a new language, writing, modern fighting tactics, roads,

public baths, town halls, tax collectors, country houses, public entertainment and a new style of dress. Sons of chieftains who had put up a heroic fight against the Romans were soon eager to learn Latin, drink wine and swagger around in Roman dress.

For four centuries, Britain prospered as an outpost of Rome's Empire. Even when the Romans went, and their towns crumbled into moss-grown ruins, they left a legacy still discernible – 1,600 years later – in overgrown stone walls, arrow-straight roads we still drive along and ancient towns where we shop. Though much of Roman Britain was obliterated by later generations of conquerors and builders, traces of it survive under modern streets – just as beneath our ever-changing culture lie the foundations of civilization laid by the first colonizers from Rome.

THE ROMAN EMPIRE

The Romans brought their imperial style and way of life to all parts of the Empire.

ROMAN MOSAIC

The Romans brought to Britain new kinds of art and interior decoration. Some fine mosaics have survived the centuries, like this example at Cirencester.

BRITAIN'S MOST FAMOUS ROMAN MONUMENT ...

... is, of course, Hadrian's Wall. Britons living south of this spectacular barrier were able – in the words of the 18th-century historian Edward Gibbon – to share 'the honours and advantages' of being Roman.

BRITAIN'S 'BARBARIANS'

> 'All Gaul is full of Roman citizens; not a single sesterce [a Roman coin] changes hands without being entered in the account books of Roman citizens.'
>
> *Cicero, Roman politician (106–43 BC)*

KINGS OF THE CATUVELLAUNI

Cassivellaunus

(in power 54 BC)

Tasciovanus

(in power *c.* 20 BC–AD 5)

Cunobelinus

(in power *c.* AD 5–42)

Togodumnus	**Caratacus**	**Adminius**
(d. AD 43)	(d. after AD 51 in Rome)	(fled to Romans in AD 39)

WHEN JULIUS CAESAR'S Roman army sailed to Britain in 55 BC, war-painted warriors lined the coastal cliff tops, ready for battle with the invaders. Caesar described these Celts as 'savage barbarians', but they were much more than that. Theirs was an organized society, with laws, hierarchy and exquisite skills in metalwork. They were personally fastidious, superstitious, poetic but without writing, and their pride and wealth lay in cattle, horses and hunting dogs. In battle they were fearsomely, heroically brave.

Caesar already knew his enemy. The British Celts were a fringe society, belonging to an ancient people rooted in central European history. Spreading across the Continent, the early Celts had split into different tribal groups with a shared inheritance of language, customs and culture. The Greeks around 500 BC knew them as 'Keltoi'. To the Romans they were 'Galli' (Gauls). Celts domi-nated west and central Europe, but they were crushed by Roman armies in 225 BC at Telamon in Tuscany. By 58 BC, when Julius Caesar began campaigning against them, the shrinking band of 'free' Celts centred on Gaul.

In his war reports, Caesar mentions Celtic settlements in south-east Britain – and this remains the only written evidence for Celtic migration to the British Isles. Archaeology, however, tells us that Celts had lived there for centuries. Now Rome's greatest general had arrived to add further laurels to his victor's crown. The warships of Europe's mighty superpower poured out their crack troops onto British soil. But the Celts also faced an onslaught from the cultural juggernaut of Rome. Seductive and implacable, it was a force that few were able to resist.

DORSET DEFENCE

Maiden Castle in Dorset was one of the great hill forts of the British. Such sites were strong-holds and rallying points for the local people. The Celts were not by nature urban dwellers.

CELTIC RULE

Britain's pre-Roman rulers were Celtic chieftain-kings. The family of the south's most powerful king, Cunobelinus, played an important part in the conflict with Rome.

DYING CELT

The 'Dying Gaul', a marble copy of a famous 2nd-century BC bronze statue, is in the Capitoline Museum in Rome. The warrior is in fact a Galatian from Turkey, but nonetheless a typical Celtic fighting man, with spiky lime-washed hair and naked apart from the torc (ring) around his neck.

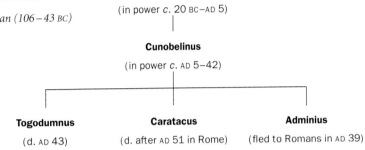

A LAND WORTH WINNING

LAND OF MIST AND MYSTERY was how Britain appeared to the Romans' Mediterranean eyes. Yet these remote, wooded isles had already been visited in the past by intrepid travel writers of the ancient world – and were a regular point of call for traders buying tin. The islands first recorded as Ierne (Ireland) and Albion (Britain) were given the name 'Prettania' in about 325 BC by Pytheas, a Greek voyager. 'Prettania' later surfaced as the Roman 'Britannia'.

Celtic farmers had been working the soils of Britain for centuries before Belgic peoples from Celtic lands across the Channel made their homes in the south-east during the last century BC. The adaptable Celts had always been quick to adjust their farming and building techniques to suit the lands they settled: in Gaul, they planted vines to make wine, as well as olives. And in Britain, these Iron-Age farmers proved just as resourceful. Most lived in scattered, isolated farming communities. Their farmsteads, with granaries, storage pits, workshops and animal pens, were protected by earth banks reinforced with wattle fencing and a ditch to keep out intruders, raiders or marauding wild animals – such as the wolves that still roamed Britain.

FARMING COMMUNITY

Part of a Celtic farm settlement reconstructed at Butser Ancient Farm, Hampshire. Thatched, circular houses and animal pens are clustered together.

Farmers could turn heavy soils with the iron-shod ploughs they dragged crossways over small, squarish fields, measuring around 120 by 80 metres (394 by 262 feet). As well as wheat, oats and rye, they grew barley for brewing their staple drink of beer, rape for oil, hemp for fibre, flax for linen, and a variety of vegetables including peas, beans, lentils and vetch (fodder). Meat and a kind of porridge would have been the basic diet.

People coppiced forest trees, cutting the timber for building, fencing and fuel. For food, milk and leather they kept cattle, pigs and small, goat-like sheep with coarse wool, which they spun and wove into weatherproof clothes and cloaks dyed in bright colours and patterns.

A century before the Roman invasion in AD 43, British farmers cleared more woodland, drained heavy clay soils, bred bigger cattle herds, and perhaps began rotating crops. The countryside the Romans saw is still, in places, familiar – woods, meadows, small fields within ditches, walls or hedges. Traces of Celtic fields, cattle folds, droveways, ditches and enclosed villages linger over the chalk downland of southern Britain. The hard work of British farmers had made their land a prize the Romans thought worth taking.

FARMERS ON GUARD

Celtic farmers lived in fear of attack from warlike neighbours, and defended their hilltop settlements with ramparts and rows of sharp stones, like these at Pen-y-Gaer (Llanbedr-y-Cennin, Conwy, North Wales).

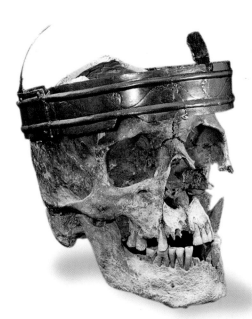

CROWNING GLORY

A skull found at Deal, Kent, dates from c. 200–100 BC. Buried with sword and shield, the body to which the skull belonged may have been that of a warrior. But the bronze crown, replicated here, may also signify that the burial was that of a chief or priest.

9

IN ENEMY TERRITORY

IN GAUL, CAESAR FOUND that Celts often chose to live 'surrounded by forest … for to avoid the heat they generally seek the neighbourhood of woods and rivers.' Heat may not have posed such a problem in Britain. The favoured location for British homeowners seeking security was a hilltop settlement.

❧

Romans discovered British Celts living in round, thatched houses with walls made from wattle (woven twigs) and daub (mud cement) in the lowlands, and from dry stone in hilly regions. Their homes were usually clustered inside a circular earth bank topped by a palisade (fence) of stakes or a stone wall, and further protected by an outer ditch.

❧

Small, scantily defended villages proved little trouble to the Romans. The network of hill forts was a different matter. Some dated from the Bronze Age and, rebuilt over many centuries, provided places of safety at times of inter-tribal warfare. Large forts – like Danebury in Hampshire and Maiden Castle – were bustling villages with 150 or more huts, where hundreds of people lived, worked, traded and kept their animals. Other settlements, varying in size and nature, included un-walled villages, religious meeting sites, or even 'industrial areas' like salt works in coastal East Anglia, or trading centres such as Hengistbury Head in Dorset.

❧

Largest of all were the tribal capitals, such as Camulodunum (Colchester), which Caesar called an *oppidum* (town) – the name used by Romans for settlements in Gaul that were larger than a village (*vicus*) or farmstead. *Oppida* grew in number as

LAKESIDE RETREAT
Water offered extra protection, a transport route and fishing. This home, reconstructed on Scotland's Loch Tay, stands on an artificial island called a crannog. Now submerged, the remains of the original settlements reveal much about Celtic life, as do other waterside settlements such as Glastonbury lake village.

The remains of Cytiau'r Gwyddelod Iron-Age hut circle on the side of Holyhead Mountain, Anglesey.

Celtic society became more centralized, with fewer but more powerful tribes.

SIMPLICITY AT HOME

The hearth was the focal point of a Celtic home. People sat around open fires, as in this reconstruction at Castell Henlys in Pembrokeshire. Wrought-iron firedogs support a cooking pot suspended from a roof-chain. Food would also have been baked in a clay oven by the fire.

To a Roman, Celtic home life must have appeared comfortless, especially in winter. The Celtic hut had a dirt floor, a low circular wall, a roof sitting on top like a high hat that almost touched the ground, and a doorway but no window. Inside, it was dark and smoky. Animal skins supplied some warmth and comfort, as did the central fireplace where a peat or log blaze heated the family stew in a cauldron suspended above it. Smoke filtered out slowly through the thatch. What little furniture the family had was wooden and simple, though Celtic metalwork displayed a high level of technical and artistic skill.

11

Hill forts

Welsh mountain stronghold

Tre'r Ceiri on Yr Eifl, on the Welsh Lleyn Peninsula, is among the most impressive of British hill forts, and one of the highest. Its largely intact walls once enclosed a village of 150 huts.

In Britain, Romans found no towns to match those of Italy, Greece or Spain. The land's biggest tribal settlements, such as the Trinovantes' capital Camulodunum, were little more than oversized villages, frequently rebuilt and extended.

British building energies had gone into hill forts, piled up from soil and rock. Hundreds were created all over the British Isles – almost 600 in Wales, over 800 in England. Born out of the Celts' warlike nature, some forts provided refuges into which people and beasts crowded when danger threatened. Some had permanent populations, but others were probably activated only in war, as bases for raiding bands or as chieftains' strongholds. Huge labour forces were organized to build these massive structures – still imposing today – with walls hundreds of metres long, up to 3 metres (9 feet) thick, and

> *'It is their custom, when they are formed for battle, to step out in front of the line and to challenge the most valiant men from among their opponents to single combat, brandishing their weapons in front of them to terrify their adversaries.'*
>
> *Diodorus Siculus, writing in the 1st century BC about the Celts*

4 metres (13 feet) high or more. They were formidable to attack – even for the Romans.

Its position and nature made a hill fort naturally hard to capture. The site provided a commanding lookout post, allowing villagers time to herd their animals inside the walls before an enemy could rush the defences. These centred on an elaborately designed gateway, with walls forming long narrow passages. The gateway was overlooked by a raised gatehouse from which defenders could hurl stones down on their enemies below. Some forts, such as Pen-y-Gaer in Conwy, Wales, had three ramparts and rows of sharp, pointed stones, like dragons' teeth, to impede the enemy – the Iron-Age equivalent of razor-wire defences.

A Celtic ruler gloried in the size and complexity of his defences, enlarging any forts won by conquest. The Trinovantes'

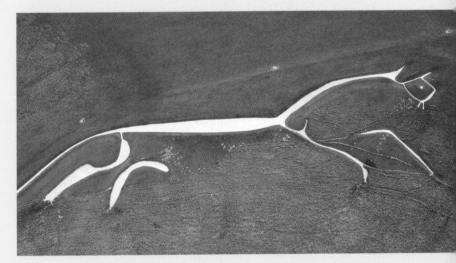

capital at Camulodunum fell to their powerful Catuvellauni rivals in the early years AD. Trusting to defensive earthworks, ditches and natural valleys, the people of Camulodunum and other tribal strongholds – the Durotriges' massive fort at Maiden Castle and that of the Brigantes at Stanwick – felt secure. But they were about to face the sternest test of all: assault by the legions of Rome.

ENIGMATIC EQUINE

Scoured from chalky downland, the White Horse at Uffington in Berkshire may have been a tribal emblem or cult symbol of the Belgic people. Some claim it to be even older than the nearby hill fort of Uffington Castle (6th or 5th century BC).

HORNED GOD OF WAR

A Celtic war god, brandishing sword and shield.

GEARED UP FOR WAR

War was part of the Celtic way of life. Time and energy were lavished on weapons and military equipment. Helmets worn by warriors in battle made them look more fearsome – Diodorus Siculus, writing in the 1st century BC, said they lent 'the appearance of enormous stature to the wearer'. Usually made of leather, some were decorated with metal and bore animal crests, often a bird or boar. Many Celts disdained armour completely.

BATTLE CLANS

A LORDLY GAME
A rich games-player of the 1st century BC was buried with pieces from his favourite pastime. The glass counters formed sets of four colours, as in the modern game of ludo.

'CIVILIZED' ROMANS SCORNED 'barbarian' Celts – yet were fascinated by their strange customs, savage energy and tactical skill in battle. Bravery, pride, boastfulness, hospitality, unpredictability and quickness to take offence were all part of the enemy's profile. Celts were also renowned drinkers of wine and ale.

Romans used their knowledge of Celtic society in planning the takeover of Britain. 'Divide and rule' was not hard to accomplish. Celtic family groups, or clans, belonged to large tribal federations that were constantly changing alliances. Heading each group was a king or chieftain, elected from the leading families and backed by a tribal council of nobles – the strong and wealthy. Prestige and rank were won and held by the taking of battle-plunder. Only freemen were protected by the law and joined tribal assemblies: the unfree worked as 'bondsmen', could not own animals or property, and were little more than slaves. A dependent – an individual or a smaller tribe – served a strong ruler in return for protection.

Successful warriors attracted a following, and Celtic lords – famed for hospitality and generosity – gave out rewards to their retainers, thereby confirming their respective places in the tribal pecking order. Gift-giving often took place at wild and drunken feasts, where the tribesmen sat by rank around their chieftain. Status within the band might be tested as they gorged on pork and swilled beer. For example, the 'hero's portion'

'They invite strangers to their feasts and do not inquire until after the meal who they are.' Diodorus Siculus, 1st-century BC Greek historian

14

of meat (such as a whole roast pig) belonged to the tribe's bravest warrior, but if a rival rose to claim it, the two men might fight to the death to prove the point.

Women married at around 14. Approximately 50 per cent of children died before they were 12, though child-graves are rare – probably because deaths were so common. Adults were often buried with jewellery, clothes or food, for use in the afterlife or as an example of their disposable wealth. Cremation was introduced to Britain from Gaul in the last decades BC, when grave goods included fine metalwork, such as iron firedogs, pottery and wine vessels.

Just as some Britons were familiar with the Roman world across the ocean, so the Romans were well aware of Celtic divisions. Britons with grievances against their own or other clan leaders had more than once found their way to Rome, begging for aid. Wily imperial politicians played off one tribe against the other, rewarding submission to weaken independence. Power-sharing with Rome generally ended with power loss, as British chieftains ruefully discovered.

CELTIC RACEGOERS

The Celts loved horses and horse racing. This pony cap, from Torrs in Scotland, was worn to protect the animal's head when racing. It was made during the 3rd or 2nd century BC – the curling horns are a later addition, the reused terminals of drinking horns.

HORSE GODDESS

The horse goddess Epona, shown on a terracotta relief from France. Epona's was a popular cult in Britain and Gaul. She was patroness of mares and foals, of cavalry and travellers on horseback.

MIRROR, MIRROR…

Fastidious – even vain – Celts lavished their artistic skill on highly polished bronze mirrors, like this 1st-century example from Desborough, Northamptonshire. The swirling pattern style developed in Britain during the 2nd and 1st centuries BC.

15

An enemy divided

Unisex jewellery

This brooch, probably intended for an Iberian ruler, was created by a Greek over 200 years before the Roman conquest of Britain. It shows a naked Celtic warrior (left) with his hunting dog. The man once had a sword (the blade is now missing) as well as his helmet and shield.

CELTIC BRITAIN HAD no one dominant power. Tribal strength ebbed and flowed with the tide of battles lost and won. At the time of the first clash with the Romans, south-east Britain's leading peoples were the Trinovantes, the Catuvellauni and the Iceni. Along the south coast of Britain lay the lands of the Cantiaci, the Regni, the Belgae, the Durotriges and – in the far west – the Dumnonii.

The Midlands was home to the Dobunni, Cornovii and Coritani. Ruling the north were the wide-ranging Brigantes, with the Parisii on the east coast. Wales had its own jigsaw of tribes: Silures, Demetae, Ordovices, Deceangli. In Scotland there were even more.

Some tribes, such as the Brigantes and Dumnonii, had held their lands for generations. But there were immigrants too, with knowledge of the Roman world. Among them were the Belgae, who kept up cross-Channel links with their cousins in Gaul – a huge region including present-day France, Belgium and Germany west of the Rhine. The west-country Dumnonii, living in what is now Cornwall, traded with the seafaring Veneti, who sailed from coastal strong-holds in present-day Brittany.

Through trade and family contacts, some British Celts were well aware of events in Gaul, where independent Celtic territory had been shrinking since the 200s BC as it fell inex-orably into the clutches of Rome. In the 50s BC, the Roman grip tightened.

From 58 BC, Julius Caesar set out to put what remained of 'free Gaul' under Roman rule. Although led by the able war-chief-tain, Vercingetorix, the Gauls fatally failed to unite, and in 52 BC were defeated at Alesia by a supremely skilful Roman siege. Then came the savage crushing of a Veneti uprising and the execution of all its leaders. News of the successive Gallic defeats arrived in Britain with traders and refugees, including Veneti seeking a safe haven from Roman vengeance. Britons along the south coast kept a close eye on the restless Channel waters, and in 55 BC the lookouts on duty at last had news to report – Roman sails.

COIN HOARD

Found in 2003 in a Leicestershire field, a hoard of around 3,000 Iron-Age gold and silver coins was the biggest yet unearthed in Britain. The shallow pit-burials were probably made between AD 1 and 40, by local people as offerings to their gods. A shattered Roman silver-gilt ceremonial helmet, found with the coins, is more intriguing. Unlikely to have been a trophy – since it is too fine for wearing in battle – could it have been a gift to a Celtic warrior-ally from the Romans?

Britain's Tribes

THE TRUMPET BLAST

Celtic battles resounded to the blast of war trumpets. This decorated mouth roundel comes from an Irish bronze trumpet, probably from the 1st century BC. Roman generals ordered troops to ignore the din.

Lugi

Caerenii

Cornovii

Smertae

Decantae

Carnonacae

Taexali

Vacomagi

Creones

CALEDONIAN
CONFEDERACY

Caledones

Venicones

Epidii

Damnonii

Votadini

Carvetii

Selgovae

Novantae

Brigantes

Parisii

Deceangli

Coritani

Ordovices

Cornovii

Iceni

Demetae

Dobunni

Catuvellauni

Trinovantes

Silures

Atrebates

Cantiaci

Belgae

Regni

Durotriges

Dumnonii

THE BRITISH TRIBES

The main tribal groups in pre-Roman Britain. Southerners had some contact with the Roman world before the invasions of Caesar and Claudius. People in the far north mostly carried on regardless of Roman ways, even after the invaders established their province of 'Britannia'.

0   50 miles

0   100 km

BRITAIN BECOMES BRITANNIA

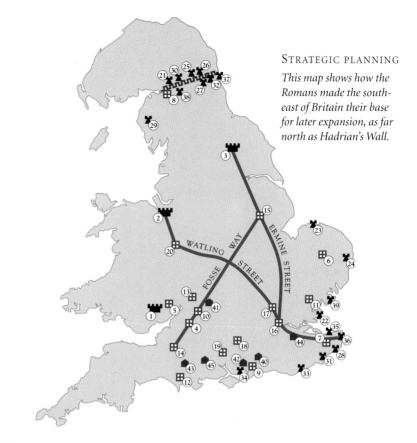

STRATEGIC PLANNING

This map shows how the Romans made the south-east of Britain their base for later expansion, as far north as Hadrian's Wall.

JULIUS CAESAR HAD MIXED motives for sailing to Britain. The prime one was political. An easy conquest would be another feather in his cap, a good career move for an ambitious politician set on achieving power in Rome and anxious to match the victories in the east of his main rival, Pompey. A quick campaign with few losses would neatly cap Rome's – that is, Caesar's – successes in Gaul.

There were arguable military reasons for invading Britain. Celts were Celts, and British Celts had been noted fighting in Gaul beside their tribal allies. Such temerity had to be punished. There were potential economic gains, too. Britain's mineral wealth would be useful to Rome, and its farmers grew good corn. Less encouraging were reports on the climate: 'objectionable, with frequent rain and mists', according to Tacitus (who never visited Britain).

As events turned out, Caesar's 55 and 54 BC expeditions were little more than raids. The Roman army gained useful intelligence about Britain, and Caesar won his triumph. Yet no follow-up invasion was launched for almost a century. Caesar's peace agreements and

ROMAN RICHBOROUGH

Richborough (Rutupiae) in Kent, recreated here by artist Ivan Lapper, was the Roman gateway to Britain and for many years the chief Roman naval base in the south.

LEGIONARY FORTRESSES
(permanent)
1 Caerleon *Isca*
2 Chester *Deva*
3 York *Eboracum*

FORTRESSES AND TOWNS
4 Bath *Aquae Sulis*
5 Caerwent *Venta Silurum*
6 Caistor *Venta Icenorum*
7 Canterbury *Durovernum Cantiacorum*
8 Carlisle *Luguvalium*
9 Chichester *Noviomagus*
10 Cirencester *Corinium*

11 Colchester *Camulodunum*
12 Dorchester *Durnovaria*
13 Gloucester *Glevum*
14 Ilchester *Lindinis*
15 Lincoln *Lindum*
16 London *Londinium*
17 St Albans *Verulamium*
18 Silchester *Calleva Atrebatum*
19 Winchester *Venta Belgarum*
20 Wroxeter *Viroconium Cornoviorum*

FORTS
21 Birdoswald *?Banna*
22 Bradwell *Othona*
23 Brancaster *Branodunum*

24 Burgh *Gariannorum*
25 Carrawburgh *Brocolitia*
26 Chesters *Cilurnum*
27 Corbridge *Corstopitum*
28 Dover *Dubris*
29 Hardknott *Mediobogdum*
30 Housesteads *Vercovicium*
31 Lympne Portus *Lemanis*
32 Newcastle-upon-Tyne *Pons Aelius*
33 Pevensey *Anderida*
34 Portchester *?Portus Adurni*
35 Reculver *Regulbium*
36 Richborough *Rutupiae*
37 South Shields *Arbeia*
38 Vindolanda
39 Walton Castle

VILLAS
40 Bignor
41 Chedworth
42 Fishbourne
43 Hinton St Mary
44 Lullingstone
45 Rockbourne

Hadrian's Wall

the resulting closer ties between some British rulers and the Roman world seemed to satisfy Roman appetites. Ironically, it was another politician's desire for a 'feel-good factor' that spurred the Romans' return. That politician was the bumbling, stuttering but shrewd Emperor Claudius, and it was he who launched the decisive attack on Britain in AD 43. When the Romans came in earnest, not even a hill fort as mighty as Maiden Castle could halt the advance of marching legions.

CLAUDIUS COIN

A coin bearing the muscular-looking head of Emperor Claudius. This scholarly, middle-aged man had ruled Rome for just two years before ordering the conquest of Britain.

CRUSHING THE CELTS

BATTLE-HARDENED ROMANS had faced Celtic armies in Gaul and elsewhere, and knew just what to expect from the Britons. First came a blood-curdling display – of screaming war cries, clashing swords on shields, blasting horns and trumpets. When worked up to a terrifying tempo, the Celts charged, wild hair streaming, swords flailing. Some wore armour and helmets, others only tunics and breeches. Warriors at the fore-front – the 'death or glory' brigade – displayed blue-dyed patterns on their naked flesh as they fought wearing nothing but a sword belt and gold neck torc.

In battle, every Celt strove for personal glory. The result was a brave but impetu-ous rabble, not a disciplined fighting force of the Roman kind. Most men fought on foot, but the Celts were good horsemen, too. Using light cavalry to harry an enemy, they surprised the Romans by their dashing deployment of two-horse chariots. Chariot warfare encouraged Celtic machismo, the most daring warriors balancing between the racing

'The whole race … is madly fond of war, high spirited and quick to battle … they are ready to face danger even if they have noth-ing on their side but their own strength and courage.'

Strabo, 1st-century Greek historian

'They fight separately and separately are defeated.'

Tacitus, 1st-century Roman historian

NAKED AND FIT FOR THE FRAY

This warrior figure from Italy originally had a shield and probably a throwing spear. He wears only a torc, weapon belt and horned helmet. Celts were proud of their physiques: Strabo notes that 'they endeavour not to grow fat or pot-bellied, and any young man who exceeds the standard measure of the girdle is punished.'

Believing that the human soul was in a person's head, Celtic warriors took home heads of enemies killed in battle as trophies. In Gaul, victorious warriors nailed heads to the door-posts of their huts. No doubt this swelled the head-hunter's status. It may also have reassured superstitious victors that the souls of dead enemies would not rise up to haunt them. Prisoners captured alive faced a lifetime of slavery.

horses, feet braced on the draught-pole. After hurling his javelins, a warrior sprang down to fight on foot with his long, slashing sword, while his charioteer left the fray – hurtling back into the mêlée to pick up his man and carry him elsewhere. Celtic armies seemed to disdain command structure: the wild din of horns and raucous yells was to dismay the enemy rather than give signals. The Celts relied on psychology, shock, awe and suicidal courage.

In Britain, the contest between Celts and invading Roman legions was to be a clash of opposites. Celts, who for centuries had fought for glory amongst themselves – tribe against tribe, champion against champion – now faced sustained, disciplined pressure from a ruthlessly purposeful foe. Tight-ranked and heavily armoured, Rome's troops were sustained by logistics that no army in the ancient world could match.

MAGICAL SWORD

The Celt's iron sword was given added potency by the smith's magic, and by personalized decoration to add charms against misfortune. This spectacular 3rd-century BC sword, from Kirkburn in Yorkshire, was crafted from over 70 parts and enamelled in scarlet. With a blade 57 centimetres (22 inches) long, it had been buried with a warrior.

TOO GOOD FOR FIGHTING

The magnificent 'Battersea' shield, found in the Thames, was made in the 2nd century BC. It was perhaps meant for display, or created as a ritual offering, before being cast into the river.

CAESAR'S WARS

ON THE NIGHT OF 25 AUGUST 55 BC, a Roman fleet of 80 ships carried 10,000 men across the Straits of Dover. As dawn broke, Caesar could see the Celts in full battle array, massed along the gleaming white chalk cliffs. The British were forewarned, and ready. Caesar wrote later, 'It was clearly no place to attempt a landing.'

The Romans sailed on eastwards to a shallow beach (near the present Walmer Castle), tailed by the British warriors. At first, Caesar's legionaries – many of them probably seasick – refused to leave their ships. Afraid to wade ashore in deep water, weighed down by armour and weapons, they faced the alarming sight of British chariots churning up the water between them and the beach.

ROMAN TROOPSHIPS
Ships crammed with soldiers appear in this detail from Trajan's Column in Rome, a copy of which is in London's Victoria and Albert Museum. The weather and Channel tides posed problems for the Romans trying to land in Britain.

Outlandish Celtic taunts echoed across the waves. Chariots were considered old-fashioned in mainland Europe, and few Roman soldiers among the expeditionary force had ever encountered them.

Caesar reacted smartly, ordering his oared war-galleys inshore alongside the transports to bombard the British with slings,

through the surf to do battle. It was a bloody landing: 'a good deal of confusion ensued,' commented the commander. But when the legions formed up and charged, the Britons were driven back.

After this initial skirmish, the Celts sought a ceasefire, sending a delegation to apologize for any 'misunderstanding' on the part of their over-zealous warriors. Caesar demanded hostages and peace was agreed. But the Channel's storms and high tides took the Romans by surprise. Ships were sunk or waterlogged, cavalry could not land, and the infantry – short of supplies – was confined to camp. Encouraged by these signs of Roman vulnerability,

COIN OF CAESAR

A coin with the head of Julius Caesar, one of the few made during his lifetime with the likeness of the general who stamped his authority on Rome, and came twice to Britain.

arrows and artillery catapults. The onslaught worked: the British fell back. Shamed by a lone standard-bearer jumping into the sea, the Romans waded

the Britons returned to attack, but were again repulsed. After four weeks, Caesar prudently withdrew to Gaul, but was already planning his return.

FOLLOW THE STANDARD

The standard was a Roman legion's honoured emblem. And the 10th Legion's standard-bearer proved the hero of the hour when his bravery inspired nervous comrades to defy the choppy Channel waters and confront the waiting British. Caesar reports him shouting: **'Come on, men! Jump, unless you want to betray your standard to the enemy. I, at any rate, shall do my duty to my country and my commander.'** Leaping over the ship's side, he then headed for the beach – followed by men with swords drawn, cheering wildly.

ROMANS RETURN

THE SECOND EXPEDITION was much larger: 800 ships according to Caesar, with 5 legions (at least 30,000 troops) and 2,000 cavalry. This time, Caesar's plan may have been to make Britain a Roman province. His troops landed in early July 54 BC, and were unopposed. No chariots were waiting on the beach: prisoners brought in by scouting parties admitted that the British had withdrawn on seeing such a huge fleet approach. Leaving behind men to dig in and guard the ships, Caesar marched north, defeated the forces that challenged his advance and, at some point,

COIN OF THE GREAT KING
This gold coin of Cunobelinus, carrying the Celtic leader's name, was probably struck at a mint in his capital, Camulodunum.

crossed the Thames. To achieve any control of southern Britain, he had to beat the Catuvellauni, whose tactically aware leader Cassivellaunus was struggling to build a tribal coalition to fight the invader under his leadership.

Yet again British weather wreaked havoc with their ships, but the Romans had at least safely landed their cavalry, making British war-chariots less of a threat. According to Caesar, Cassivellaunus abandoned any hope of winning a set-piece battle and instead used his 4,000 chariots to harry the Roman advance, driving off cattle and burning crops to deprive the legions of food. 'Scorched-earth' tactics backed up by lightning chariot attacks might have forced a Roman retreat, but Cassivellaunus must have

ROMANS RETURN
A modern Briton, Romanized to re-enact the battles of 2,000 years ago.

been disheartened by double-dealing and treachery around him. As so often before, the Celts could not forget festering grievances. The Trinovantes, old enemies of the Catuvellauni, made a separate peace deal with the Romans. Other tribes, maybe sensing the way the wind was blowing, decided to do the same.

Cassivellaunus fell back on a tribal stronghold, possibly near Wheathampstead in Hertfordshire, but the Romans – old hands at siege warfare – stormed his fort on two sides. 'After a very brief resistance,' wrote Caesar, 'the enemy gave way and escaped … Great quantities of cattle were found there and many of the fugitives were over-taken and killed.' Cassivellaunus made peace. Caesar took hostages, imposed taxes and sailed back to Gaul, where the army's absence had encouraged a new round of fierce Celtic resistance.

So ended Rome's first invasion of Britain. In the follow-ing decades, Roman camps decayed and Celts returned to their squabbling. But contact had been made. Trade grew between Britain and the Roman world. Some British rulers took to stamping *rex* (Latin for king) on their coins. From about AD 10, Cunobelinus of the Catuvellauni (Shakespeare's Cymbeline) was the most powerful of British rulers. Even the Trinovantes, staunch allies of Rome, submitted to him at his capital of Camulodunum. It was a son of Cunobelinus – named Adminius – who fled banishment and turned up in Rome in AD 39, wanting the emperor Caligula to invade Britain. A force was assembled, though it never sailed. But before long, tangled British politics were about to open up a new opportunity for Rome.

BIRD-WING SHIELD BOSS

This elegant piece of Iron-Age metalwork, on which bird wings loop in curling tendrils, once formed the centrepiece of a Celtic shield. Made probably in the century before the Romans came, it was found in the River Thames at Wandsworth, London.

ICENI GOLD

Gold torcs from a hoard buried at Snettisham in Norfolk 2,000 years ago show the startling wealth of British Iceni nobles. Torcs were symbols rather than accessories, so fascinating the Romans that they awarded torcs to their own soldiers for bravery.

25

Claudius conquers

Four legions were ordered to join the invasion fleet: the 2nd Augusta, 14th Gemina, 20th Valeria and 9th Hispana. With auxiliary troops and support units, the Roman army numbered close on 50,000. Its commander was Aulus Plautius, who landed his force in divisions: one at Richborough, the others probably at Dover and Lympne. According to the historian Dio Cassius, the Romans had problems bringing the British to battle: the natives 'took refuge in the swamps and forests, hoping to wear out the invaders.' But the two forces met on the banks of the Medway, where after fighting for two days the British retreated north across the Thames. One of their two chieftains, Togodumnus, died fighting or from wounds – perhaps even as the Romans crossed the river into what is now Essex.

WAR WAGON

Celtic charioteers taxied their noble warriors at breakneck speed to whichever part of the battlefield they were needed.

IN AD 41, CLAUDIUS became emperor of Rome, following the murder of the crazy Caligula. But when Cunobelinus died in Britain the following year, his two sons Caratacus and Togodumnus showed no deference towards the new Roman ruler. Yet another British exile, King Verica of the Atrebates – forced out by Cunobelinus – begged Rome's help in seeking vengeance. Claudius saw his chance to seize glory from Celtic confusion. Responding to Verica's plea, in AD 43 he launched a new Roman invasion fleet across the Channel.

The invasion was Rome's D-Day – a seaborne assault that would crush the dangerous spread of Catuvellaunian power. Conquest would also seize Britain's wealth, push the imperial frontier northwards, and end the island's role as a haven for Gallic freedom fighters.

Camulodunum was theirs for the taking, but instead the army halted for perhaps six weeks. Caratacus was given time to slip away westward. Why the delay? Plautius possibly needed time to rest and regroup, but he was also obeying imperial command. Claudius wanted his share of the glory. Summoned by urgent courier, the emperor 'hurried' (in imperial state, with appropriate stops for refreshment) from Rome. Claudius and his retinue took ship to Marseilles, trekked across Gaul, made the short sea crossing to Kent, then trundled across downland, marsh and mudflats to Camulodunum. There the emperor accepted surrender from those British leaders who had thrown in their lot with the invader. Resplendent in armour, the lame, stuttering, scholarly Claudius entered triumphant into his conquest at the head of his troops, riding on an elephant.

~

The emperor stayed in Britain for just 16 days, to receive submission from tribal leaders. Ordering Plautius to finish the task of subjugation, Claudius then returned to Rome for further celebrations. It was to take the Romans 90 more years to 'finish the task' of pacifying England and Wales. Scotland was never subdued, nor did the Romans land in force on Irish soil. Though the Roman historian Suetonius dismissed the emperor's role – 'he fought no battle nor did he suffer any casualties' – Claudius had his triumph. He was given the title 'Britannicus' by the Senate: another province had been added to membership of the Roman Empire.

EMPEROR CLAUDIUS
A marble bust of Claudius, crowned in triumph.

ASSAULT TROOPS

As these retro-Romans charge, it is easy to sympathize with the Britons. Roman infantry advanced in lines behind a wall of shields, hurling javelins before rushing in to cut down the enemy with their short, stabbing swords.

FRIENDS AND FOES

ROME'S TRIUMPH HAD BEEN dramatically fast. By the time Claudius set sail for Gaul to review his troops on the Rhine before returning to Rome, the new province was practically his.

The Catuvellauni had so nearly beaten him to it. Now their mini-empire of southern Britain had been snatched away by a much mightier power but, still licking their wounds, they had not yet given up hope. Their war-chieftain Caratacus, on the run with his followers, was rallying support for a counter-attack.

Making a tactical retreat to the far west, into Wales, Caratacus and his men sought refuge with the warlike Silures and Ordovices. According to the Roman Tacitus, these tribes still 'dreaded peace with us' and in their lands the Romans remained a very distant threat. The escaping Catuvellauni warriors must have brought thoroughly unwelcome news along with their tales of heroic resistance.

Caratacus had learned a lot about Roman methods and endurance from his first encounter with the legions. He knew that the British, flinging whooping sword-whirlers into action and charging from thundering chariots, were no match for Roman troops in a set-piece battle. Nor were British hill forts safe from an enemy experienced in siege tactics. The Roman military machine possessed not only heavy engineering capacity, but also formidable artillery: crossbows and

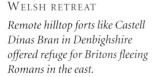

WELSH RETREAT

Remote hilltop forts like Castell Dinas Bran in Denbighshire offered refuge for Britons fleeing Romans in the east.

Tacitus had generous praise for Caratacus 'who by many an indecisive and many a successful battle had raised himself far above all the other generals of the Britons'. The resistance leader was now fighting a guerrilla campaign, since he was 'inferior in military strength, but deriving an advantage from the deceptiveness of the country'. Tacitus was of course writing with hindsight, knowing that, however gallant, Caratacus was destined to lose.

BATTERING DOWN RESISTANCE

This relief from Trajan's Column shows Emperor Trajan leading his troops against Dacians. The battles in Britain were similar collisions between Celtic fervour and Roman rigour, and the outcomes were the same – Roman victories.

HATS ON PARADE

A Roman parade helmet and face mask from the Newstead site at Melrose in Scotland, dating from the late 1st century AD.

slingshots firing stones, bolts and other kinds of assault missiles.

Caratacus also knew that too many major British leaders had shown, by refusing to fight, a preference for Roman rule above Catuvellaunian overlordship. Eleven chieftains are said to have submitted to Claudius, though only one tribal name (belonging to the Dobunni) is recorded. Among the others, the Romans had won three key allies: Cogidubnus, overlord of the Atrebates and Regni; Prasutagus of the Iceni; and Queen Cartimandua of the northern Brigantes.

Cogidubnus – a man of unusual wealth and prestige – took power between AD 45 and 75. His headquarters were at Chichester (Noviomagus), where it is likely that he later came to occupy the most grandiose residence – the palace at Fishbourne. The support of such powerful British rulers was a significant boost to Roman consolidation of power, and made life more difficult for leaders of resistance, such as Caratacus.

LEGIONS MARCH

ROMAN ARCH

Lincoln (Lindum) grew up around the 9th Legion's fortress and was one of a network of military towns built in the wake of invasion. Although it has been repaired over the centuries, Newport Arch is the only Roman town gateway to survive virtually in its original state.

THE ROMANS CHOSE to secure the lowlands before tackling the hills, valleys and wildernesses of west and north Britain. It took less than three months for Aulus Plautius to subdue the south-east, and within four years the northern frontier line of the new province of Britannia ran roughly from Lincoln to Exeter.

The four legions of the invasion force fanned out to eliminate any patches of resistance and begin 'pacification'.

The 2nd Augusta headed west, making its base at what became Silchester. The 9th marched north, first to a base near modern Peterborough, then to Leicester (Ratae) and Lincoln (Lindum) and as far as York (Eboracum) and the River Humber. The 20th Legion seems to have stayed for some time in Camulodunum itself, where a Roman town, complete with huge temple in Claudius' honour, was soon to be built on the hill above the British settlement.

ROMAN CAVALRYMAN

The tombstone of Rufus Sita, a Roman cavalry-man of the 1st century AD. *He wields a long, lance-like spear to stab down at a fallen enemy, and from his belt hangs a long sword or* spatha.

Marching out from its south-eastern bridgehead, the army planted strings of forts along the way to serve as bases for soldiers and administrators. Some became major legionary bases. Evidence for military movements is scanty, but tombstones of 9th-Legion soldiers suggest they were in Lincoln by AD 48, moving on to York where – camped between the rivers Ouse and Foss – they laid the foundations of what became medieval England's second city. Tombstones at Wroxeter (Viroconium), in Shropshire, show the 14th Gemina were there, having marched west through the heart of Catuvellauni territory. By AD 47, the Romans had a secure grip on their fledgling province.

The best-documented campaign was the 2nd Augusta's, probably because its commander, Titus Flavius Vespasianus (Vespasian) – who went on to achieve the top job of Roman emperor – had his career highlights written up with enthusiasm by later historians.

Vespasian was no high-born noble Roman: his grandfather was a centurion and his father a money-lender in Switzerland (showing how ancient some traditions are). Success as a commander in Britain proved Vespasian's springboard to fame, and Suetonius is full of admiration: this hero, he says, 'fought 30 battles, subjugated two warlike tribes, captured more than 20 strongholds, beside the entire island of Vectris [the Isle of Wight].' But smart Romans rather enjoyed poking fun at this uncharismatic soldier, who usually wore a strained look on his face. Suetonius tells us that Vespasian asked a well-known wit, noted for his quips about the famous, to make up a joke about him. The wit's tart reply was: 'I will when you have at last finished relieving yourself.'

Vespasian was about to show his mettle. He headed west with the 2nd Augusta, into battle against the – so far – unconquered Durotriges and Belgae of Dorset and Wiltshire.

COMMON TOUCH

Vespasian, proud of his humble origins, was popular with his men. He seemed to find the excesses of imperial show tiresome, reflecting after a lavish parade to celebrate his victories: 'What an old fool I was to demand a triumph.'

DIGGING IN FOR THE NIGHT

When a marching column stopped for the night, Roman soldiers put up a camp of tents inside a ditch and mound topped by a palisade (fence) of pointed poles carried as part of their equipment. In an hour or so after throwing down their kit, a squad of well-trained legionaries could relax inside this rampart-defended camp.

THE FORT BUILDERS

FORAGING ROMANS WERE never far from a fort, whether a temporary night-camp or a permanent walled base. The fort (*castra*, in Latin – from which come Ciren*cester*, Col*chester* and other place names) was a symbol of Roman intent to stay. Hastily thrown-up constructions with turf ramparts and wooden buildings have long since disappeared; those forts rebuilt in stone – and formidable in size – not only outlasted their builders but were recycled by later generations. Roman stonework can be seen in medieval castles built a thousand years after the Romans arrived.

The main legionary fortresses – such as those at Caerleon in South Wales and at York – covered about 50 acres. The fort-plan was roughly playing-card shape, with rounded corners. Headquarters was in the centre, with a hall big enough for the whole legion to gather for pep talks and special ceremonies. There were regimental offices, a strongroom for valuables, and a

WELSH FORT

Caerleon in South Wales is one of the key Roman military sites in Britain. The remains of the Roman barracks include the legionaries' latrines.

TOP BRASS

A Roman belt buckle, worn by a soldier or government official, found at Mucking in Essex.

shrine to the emperor where the legion's standards were kept. The commander's house surrounded a courtyard and had its own bathhouse. Bathhouses for legionaries were usually inside the fortress walls, but a smaller garrison bathhouse might be sited outside them, to reduce fire-hazard from its wood-burning furnace. Inside the fort were granaries, workshops, stables and rows of barrack blocks, each housing 80 men. Along the walls ran a walkway for patrolling sentries, with guarded turrets at regular intervals.

Smaller forts of no more than 5 acres were used by auxiliary units that included British recruits. Even smaller fortlets, for detachments of up to 100 soldiers, were placed at intervals between the bigger forts. Retired soldiers (veterans) were settled in military townships (*coloniae*), the first founded at Colchester in AD 49. *Coloniae* not only provided homes for soldiers leaving the legion when their service ended, but acted as a model for local people: here were Roman citizen-soldiers living among them, peacefully farming the land. But whose land was it? As settlement continued, and more land was taken from them, the British became increasingly resentful. They disliked being conquered.

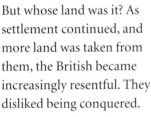

MEN AT WORK

A relief from Trajan's Column shows in detail how the legionaries turned their hands, and muscles, to fort-building.

HILL FORT RESISTANCE

AS VESPASIAN PUSHED westward, into the territory of the Durotriges, the Romans faced the challenge of rooting out the Britons from their most impressive hill forts.

Maiden Castle in Dorset saw a fierce struggle, according to such evidence as sword-savaged skeletons and iron arrowheads from a ballista – a light artillery piece. Romans were undaunted by any defences, bringing up their artillery to dislodge the enemy from hill fort ramparts. Legionaries then stormed the earthworks while torching the wooden gates. Men, women and children died as British huts burned, and the Romans took possession of one more hilltop.

Hill forts to meet a similar fate were Hod Hill and Spettisbury Rings in Dorset, as the Britons quickly learned they could do little to halt the westward advance of such determined opponents. On reaching as far as the sites of Exeter (Isca Dumnoniorum) – possibly to subdue the Dumnonii of Devon and Cornwall – and Gloucester (Glevum), Plautius decided to pause and consolidate.

Rome now controlled all Britain south of the road later called the Fosse Way, from the Severn to the Humber rivers. Garrisoned by detachments in small forts, this frontier zone formed a shield protecting the infant Roman province from attack. Client-rulers were expected to help in keeping out unwelcome intruders.

Plautius' term as Britain's first Roman governor ended in the winter of AD 47–48 and he returned

BOLT FROM THE BLUE

This ballista bolt lodged in a skeleton's vertebrae is cited as evidence of fierce fighting at Maiden Castle.

GIANT CROSSBOW

The giant crossbow, or ballista, was wound back to shoot stones, javelins or bolts. The most powerful could hurl a javelin over 400 metres (440 yards).

HOD HILL

The remains of the hill fort at Hod Hill in Dorset. This stronghold of the Durotriges tribe fell to the Romans in AD 44.

to Rome, to public acclaim. In his place came the less high-profile, but highly thought of, Publius Ostorius Scapula. Perhaps a former legionary commander, Ostorius may even have taken part in the invasion.

Governor Ostorius was soon tested. His aim – according to Roman history – was 'to tame everything this side of the Trent and Severn', presumably by disarming tribes, like the Iceni, who had welcomed the Romans. It was not a wise move. Wanting to get on with 'province-building', the Romans had yet to learn that Britain's settlement would be finalized only after further slaughter. In the renewed conflict, Romans would clash head-on with Celtic Britain's two most famous rebel leaders: Caratacus and Boudicca.

SETTLING IN

'To them [the Romans], real battles are simply manoeuvres in which blood is shed.'

Josephus, 1st-century Jewish historian

WHEN GOVERNOR PLAUTIUS returned home in AD 47, he must have felt that the conquest of Britain was all but over. 'Immediately after him [Aulus Plautius] came Ostorius Scapula, both of them excellent in the art of war: little by little the nearest part of Britain was reduced into the form of a province.' So wrote Tacitus, with approval.

In fact, it took nearly a century for the Romans to 'civilize' southern Britain, and extend control upwards to make Hadrian's Wall the northern frontier of the Roman world. Firmly encamped in the south-east, the legions had two main tasks: firstly, to root out any tribal resistance, and secondly, to entice Britons into the luxury of a Roman lifestyle – which they achieved through a town-building programme. They took over the sites of British settlements, such as Silchester (Calleva Atrebatum), the old capital of the Atrebates. Town life was the key to settlement, for although many Romans loved the countryside, they were first and foremost 'townies'. Shops, temples,

GATEWAY TO URBAN LIFE

Silchester's main gate, through which the life of the town flowed daily. Having selected and planned a site, the Romans provided some aid in building a town and setting up an administrative system. They then left the locals to run it.

bathhouses, roads – these 'blessings of civilization' were what Rome offered its colonies and their subjects.

But first came pacification, and the British were not yet under the Roman thumb. Post-invasion, the Romans met more resistance in the west, stiffened by Caratacus' leadership. Having overcome that problem, they discovered that even tribes once written off as 'pacified' could rise up in furious action if provoked. The Boudiccan revolt of AD 60–61 came as a bloody shock.

Much fighting still lay ahead, and much building. Combining attack with fortification and construction enabled the Romans to hold and mould their new province of Britannia.

GUIDING LIGHT

The Roman lighthouse at Dover (Dubris) still stands. Eight-sided, the tower was built in the 2nd century to guide merchant ships and warships of the British-Roman fleet, the Classis Britannica, which was probably based at the port. The tower was originally about 24 metres (80 feet) high, topped by a brazier burning day and night.

ROMAN COLUMN

The Romans set up camp at what is now York in AD 71, laying the foundations for the fortress-city of Eboracum. A single stone column is the last survivor of 36 columns that once supported the great hall in which much later, in AD 306, Roman troops proclaimed Constantine emperor. Part of the foundations of the garrison headquarters can be seen in the crypt of the medieval York Minster.

SUBDUING BRITAIN

THE NEW ROMAN GOVERNOR, Ostorius Scapula, found the British situation 'fluid'. Peace treaties – chiefly with powerful tribes such as the Iceni and Brigantes – did not stop Britons and Romans regarding each other with mutual suspicion. The western frontier was hazily defined, and Welsh tribes were openly aggressive, daring the Romans to advance beyond the River Severn.

Ostorius at once set out to show the Britons who was boss and to map out their future for them. Many tribespeople, stunned by the speed of invasion, now realized that the Romans were here for good. This was no 'showing the flag' exercise, like Caesar's brief expedition 90 years earlier. That had been portrayed as a British 'victory' by song-singers around smoky tribal fires. Startled Britons now saw Roman forts springing up across their land. Realization at last dawned: they had exchanged one overlord (the ambitious Catuvellauni) for another, alien power. Tribes who had made peace agreements with Rome (and those who had offered no resistance) were furious when ordered by Ostorius to disarm and hand over their

ROMAN SWORDS

The traditional Roman sword, a *gladius*, was used in a stabbing motion, thought to be more deadly than a cutting stroke. The longer *spatha*, used by the cavalry, was influenced by the long Celtic slashing sword and was easier to swing on horseback. The *spatha*, with a blade up to 80 centimetres (30 inches) long, replaced the *gladius* during the later Roman Empire.

weapons. The governor mistrusted his new allies, but his heavy-handed attempt to pre-empt revolt instead provoked it.

The Iceni of East Anglia took to their chariots. Other tribes joined the upsurge, but the rising was short-lived. Ostorius sent in lightly armoured, fast-moving auxiliaries to harry the tribes – keeping the awesome power of the legions as

back-up – and won a fenland battle, possibly near March in Cambridgeshire.

Defeat subdued Iceni anger – for the time being. But the humiliation simmered, fuelled no doubt, as months passed, by reports from the west. Ostorius had marched against the Deceangli of North Wales, swinging east to crush a minor uprising among the – until now – peaceful Brigantes. Summary executions of a few leaders were doled out as a warning to others. Yet resistance burned bright in the west, for the Silures and Ordovices had banded together under the military leadership of exiled Caratacus, the warrior-prince whose name was to pass into Welsh myth and place-name as Caradoc.

Trouble brewed, while soldiers of the Empire busily built their forts. Teams of army engineers and surveyors laid out roads between the forts, preparing a strategic infrastructure to tighten their grasp on Britain. The Romans were ready for a challenge they must have sensed was coming.

WALLED UP

Tombstone of a Roman soldier, shown wearing a long, top-buttoned cloak over a tunic fastened at the waist. The stone, reused as part of a tower in London's city wall, had probably been erected near Bishopsgate.

WHEELED RACERS

British war-chariots were built of light wickerwork, making them speedy and manoeuvrable in battle. Examples have been found in chariot-burials such as this from Garton-on-the-Wolds, in Yorkshire.

'Their territory was ravaged, spoil taken everywhere without the enemy risking battle, or if they tried to harass our march by surprise attacks, their cunning was always punished.'

Tacitus, on Ostorius' methodical generalship

39

BRITAIN'S ROMAN ROADS

The Roman road at Wheeldale in Yorkshire. Road widths varied from 6 to 9 metres (20 to 30 feet), depending on their importance. Very few British roads were paved to the same standard as roads in Rome.

BRITONS IN THE SOUTH-EAST watched with puzzled awe the physical changes made by their conquerors. For not only were Romans building forts, they were also constructing roads – of a kind new to Britain, where foot-trodden trackways had been the link between communities since ancient times.

Most of the known 13,000 kilometres (8,000 miles) of Roman roads in Britain were built in the second half of the 1st century AD – in other words, during the post-invasion settlement period. They were military roads, built by the army for the army, to move men, materials and despatches as swiftly as possible.

The first roads linked army camps, with forts set up about 24 kilometres (15 miles) apart, the regulation distance for a day's march. Later roads connected newly built towns. Britain's first main road was Watling Street (a later name), running from Richborough to Wroxeter, then west to Wales and north to Chester. Ermine Street was the main route north from London to Lincoln, and eventually to the northern border. Straightest of all straight Roman roads was the Fosse Way from Ilchester (Lindinis), through Bath (Aquae Sulis), then across country north-east to join Ermine Street at Lincoln.

Most people assume that an old straight road must be Roman. Sometimes it is.

Roman carts were usually built with wheels 143 centimetres (4 feet 8 inches) apart. Wheels wore ruts in the road, and 1,700 years later standard gauge railway track was based on the inheritance of ancient wheel ruts.

Wherever possible, Roman surveyors plotted the route from one high point to another in a straight line, but were willing to deviate around very steep inclines or marshland, or to reach a place suitable for fording a river. Cuttings went through hilltops, while steep gradients of more than one in six were surmounted by cutting zigzag terraces.

Road-building was the job of legionaries, who conscripted local gangs of labourers. The standard technique was to dig a drainage ditch either side of the marked route, and pile the spoil in between to form an embankment, known as an agger. On top were laid large stones, sometimes with a kerb, then a layer of smaller stones and gravel rammed down to give a dense surface with a camber for drainage. Gravel was the favoured top surface. Few British roads had the large paving slabs seen on Roman roads in Italy or North Africa.

All roads were marked by engraved or painted milestones, giving the distance to the next town (a Roman mile was 1,481 metres, or 1,620 yards) and some glowing words of praise for the emperor at the time. About 100 of these milestones have survived being uprooted by generations of builders. Post-houses along the main routes provided fresh horses for riders of the imperial post service and official travellers. Couriers stayed in roadside inns. A typical journey – from London to the legionary fort at Caerleon, for example – took three days, as recorded in a document called the Antonine Itinerary. This register of stations and distances from Rome along imperial roads dates from the 4th century. It gives the names of several thousand place-names in the Empire, and includes 15 routes in Roman Britain. The routes are those used by Roman officials on government business.

STRAIGHT UP

A section of the Roman Ermine Street, cut by ancient Romans and still part of the 21st-century road network.

THE LAST STAND

BRITISH RESISTANCE IN THE WEST was a guerrilla campaign fought in woods, marshes and hills. Warrior bands, operating with no unified command, attacked wherever and whenever a 'target of opportunity' arose.

〜

Caratacus was the only British leader with enough charisma to command warriors from tribes other than his own. His high rank, as son of Cunobelinus, plus his talent for diplomacy and war, gave him a unique position – and made him Rome's 'public enemy number one', the man to target. All Britons who feared or hated the Romans rallied to his cause.

〜

The Roman war-machine, marching west to confront and eliminate the danger, fought its crucial battle probably in AD 51. A one-sided Roman report from Tacitus tells of Caratacus' last stand. The British general and his allies had chosen a site where both advance and retreat would be difficult for the Romans, yet easy for their own men. Its precise whereabouts remains unknown, but must have been on the Welsh side of the River Severn. As before, the British trusted in a strip of water for their defence, and yet again the Romans proved their trust misguided by crossing the river without difficulty.

〜

The British grouped on a hillside, behind a rampart of stones. Rousing them by fiery speeches, Caratacus told his warriors that the battle would be decisive: either it would win back their freedom or condemn them to slavery.

UNDER NEPTUNE'S WATCHFUL EYE

Crossing the Severn and other British rivers, the Romans used bridge-building methods tried and tested in campaigns across Europe. A relief from Trajan's Column in Rome shows soldiers crossing the River Danube, under the protection of the water-god Neptune.

RALLYING RESISTANCE

Caratacus in heroic pose, sculpted in 1856 by John Henry Foley.

TORTOISE ATTACK

The testudo *was a reliable Roman tactic when under fire. An infantry section linked shields at the sides and over-head to protect the men beneath the 'tunnel' against stones, spears and arrows. Under cover of the* testudo, *the Romans could get close to a Celtic hill fort, and then break through the defences.*

Appeals were cried to the heroic ancestors who had sent Caesar packing a hundred years before, so preserving the sanctity of British women and children.

Ostorius Scapula's men were up to the challenge. They stormed the hillside in *testudo* (tortoise) formation, holding aloft linked shields against the hail of stones and spears flung down at them. Breaching the rampart, they tore down its stones, drove back the enemy with javelins, and then closed in with their swords. In the words of Tacitus, it was 'a glorious victory'. The brothers, wife and daughter of Caratacus were captured. The British leader again escaped, fleeing north to the lands of the Brigantes, whose queen Cartimandua then treacherously handed him over to the enemy. Caratacus was taken a chained captive to Rome, and with his farewell it seemed that the last resist-ance of south Celtic Britain had ended.

'The Romans not only easily defeat those who fight with a [Celtic] slashing sword, they laugh at them as well.' Vegetius, 4th-century military historian

CARATACUS IN ROME

Caratacus was paraded in Rome before Emperor Claudius, but the British leader's noble bearing impressed his captors. Surveying the splendid imperial city, Caratacus asked wryly, **'when you have all this, why do you envy us our poor hovels?'** To the emperor, he speculated that his noble rank might have earned him a welcome as a friend, not a prisoner. **'Does it follow that because you desire universal empire, one must accept universal slavery?'** he went on. Claudius ordered his chains struck off, allowing Caratacus and his family to live out the rest of their days as 'guests' in Rome.

Guerrilla resistance

Their own brand of magic

The aquilifer *was a key army officer, carrying the sacred eagle of the legion into battle. In this re-enactment he wears a lion-skin headdress. As Romans charged the Druids, their* aquilifer *would have been at the front along with the* imaginifer, *carrying an image of the emperor, and the* signifers, *bearing the emblems of each century.*

WITHOUT CARATACUS, the British seemed set for servitude or civilization. But a new Roman governor, Aulus Didius Gallus, replaced Ostorius, who died suddenly, in AD 52 or 53. Soon there was more trouble from unruly elements fighting guerrilla campaigns from remote strongholds.

The Silures were still picking off Romans from the Welsh mountains and now, from across the Pennines, the Brigantes added to the trouble brewing. Their leader Venutius was – after Caratacus – 'the most outstanding Briton in the field of military science', according to Tacitus. But Venutius had fallen out with the pro-Romans in his loose-knit kingdom, a clique led by his wife Cartimandua. Having tired of her husband, this queen had taken a younger, possibly low-born, lover named Vellocatus and invited him to rule beside her while Venutius seethed in his own family fiefdom. Indignant at such goings-on, many people rallied to Venutius. The incensed chieftain then suffered a second insult when Cartimandua dared to take his brother hostage. Goaded beyond endurance, Venutius launched an attack at the head of a band of young hotheads. The Celts were in-fighting again.

Fearing civil war, and loss of a key ally, the Romans sent in troops who probably included the 9th Legion from its base near Peterborough. The legion did its job, the Brigantes simmered with indignation,

Cartimandua was confirmed in power and Venutius retired to lick his wounds.

In AD 54, Rome had a new emperor, Nero. The fourth governor of Roman Britain, Quintus Veranius, died around AD 58 and his successor was another tough soldier, Gaius Suetonius Paulinus. Paulinus had learned mountain fighting in North Africa, and in AD 60 he marched boldly into North Wales to attack Anglesey – called Mona by the Romans. This was the stronghold of the British priesthood, the Druids, who were fomenting resistance. Overcoming their initial fear of this magic-shrouded encounter with a mass of wild men, priests and even wilder women, the legionaries did what they did best. Victory won, the sacred Druid groves ('devoted to inhuman superstitions', according to the Romans) were laid waste and all trappings of the old religion

A Celtic home

These stones are all that remains of a house in the fortified Celtic village of Din Lligwy on Anglesey. The Romans almost completely destroyed the Druid stronghold on the island.

THE NORTH FALLS

The moorland landscape of North Yorkshire, once part of the Brigantes' territory. Tacitus says that the Brigantes were Britain's largest tribe.

put to the torch. Normally tolerant of other people's gods, the Romans feared both the mysteries and blood-sacrifices of Druidism. They were too heady a patriotic potion for people not yet pacified.

WILD WOMEN OF WALES

Tacitus wrote a famous description of the Roman encounter with Druids on Anglesey. 'On the shore stood the opposing army with its dense array of armed warriors, while **between the ranks dashed women, in black attire like Furies, with hair dishevelled, waving brands. All around, the Druids, lifting up their hands to heaven and pouring forth dreadful imprecations, scared our soldiers ...** so that, as if paralysed, they stood motionless and exposed to wounds. Then urged by their general's appeals and mutual encouragements **not to quail before a troop of frenzied women, they bore the standards onwards,** smote down all resistance and wrapped the fire in the flames of his own brands.'

Druids' rites: the wrong religion for Rome

Human sacrifice?

The Celts killed humans as part of their religious rituals. This detail from the Gundestrup Cauldron (Denmark) is said to show a victim either being drowned in a filled container, or about to be pitched down a deep pit-shaft.

THE CELTS HAD AT LEAST 400 gods and goddesses – many probably the same spirit with different local names. They 'lived' in oak groves, rivers, lakes and other natural places. Ritual and magic linked the people to their nature-gods, whose favour demanded rites to be performed at selected shrines and holy places – sacred trees, springs, streams and pools, wooded groves and caves.

Their gods, so Celts believed, spoke to the tribal priests or Druids – a title linked to their word for the oak, the sacred tree. To the Druids, the gods made known their voracious appetite for sacrifice – of animals, precious objects and humans. No sacrifice meant no god-granted gifts – no health, wealth, happiness, no fertility of man or harvest, and certainly no victory in battle. Therein lay the power of

the Druids, whose magic rituals took place largely unobserved. Of temples for public worship, almost nothing has been found.

Recruited almost exclusively from the nobility, the Druids were an aloof caste, guarding their rites in secrecy, to keep their hold on oral tribal lore. It took 20 years to become a Druid, committing generations-worth of

> *'They bring thither two white bulls … Clad in a white robe, the priest ascends the [oak] tree and cuts the mistletoe with a golden sickle … They then kill the victims.'*
> Pliny, Roman writer, 1st century AD

Puffin Island off Anglesey. The isle of Anglesey was the headquarters of the Druids, and so a key target for the Roman army in AD 60.

LINDOW MAN

This extraordinary preserved corpse was uncovered from Lindow Moss, a dried-up bog near Manchester, in 1984. Theories about Lindow Man include the suggestion that he was a willing sacrificial victim, killed ritually to appease the gods and thereby save the Druids of the north-west from the advancing Roman army.

twigs, they fill with living men and set on fire'. The Roman author Lucan hinted darkly of outrages linked to rotting wooden idols and branches smeared with human blood. He observed that sacrificial death had to fulfil a particular god's demands: burning for the god Taranis; drowning for Teutates; hanging for Esus. Some deities were less bloodthirsty: there was Sul, goddess of the hot spring at Bath; Epona, the horse goddess; and the water goddess Elen. Dedications to Maponus are found around Hadrian's Wall and to Nodens in Gloucestershire. Some gods were linked in triads; others were shape-shifters, transforming into animals.

knowledge to memory, in a form of verse. All Druids were bards, though not all bards became Druids.

The Romans appeared shocked by Druid rites, even though animal sacrifice was a familiar feature of Roman life. They wrote of human sacrifice: by drowning, ritual strangling, or the burning of helpless victims pushed into 'figures of immense size, whose limbs, woven out of

Most unsettling to the Romans, however, was the Druid teaching of the transmigration of souls. Every Celtic warrior was taught that when he died, he would be born again in another body – and the Romans thought this explained their reckless bravery in battle. Fear of such 'fanaticism' may explain why the Romans, normally sympathetic to tribal religions, went out of their way to destroy the Druids.

BOUDICCA'S REVOLT

PAULINUS HAD LITTLE TIME to reflect on his success in Anglesey before news came of a revolt in the east, among the Iceni. Prasutagus, king of the Iceni, had recently died. A staunch ally of Rome, he had virtually handed over his territory as a client-state, in the hope of avoiding penalties. The reverse had happened. Heavy-handed Roman officials had not only helped themselves to tax revenues but also to Iceni nobles' homes and land. To these offences was added physical assault: allegedly the rape of the late king's daughters and the whipping of his widow, Queen Boudicca.

Rebellion erupted with startling ferocity, as Boudicca proved the focus for other discontented tribes, notably the Trinovantes. Above all, these people were inflamed by land-grabbing veteran legionaries who settled in the new *coloniae*, seizing not just nobles' land but anyone's farmland.

The great revolt of AD 61 (or 60, according to some historians) was led by the formidable Iceni warrior-queen who was seen by Romans as 'very tall … her voice was harsh … a great mass of red hair fell to her hips.' Rampaging Britons went on an orgy of slaughter. Excited by favourable omens – the fall of the Roman statue of Victory at Camulodunum and visions in sacred rivers of burning towns and slain Romans – they believed the gods were with them. A force of 200 Roman soldiers rushing to restore order was driven into Camulodunum's new temple of Claudius and slaughtered before the building went up in flames. Hurrying to the rescue, the 9th Legion was routed.

Paulinus gathered his remaining troops in London (Londinium) but, deciding it could not be defended, marched north. His withdrawal sealed the city's fate. Of the inhabitants: 'those who were chained to the spot by the weakness of their sex, or the infirmity of age,

ICENI COINS

This cache of coins found in Cambridgeshire may have been hidden during Boudicca's uprising. For whatever reason, the owner was never able to return and retrieve them.

'The enemy neither took nor sold prisoners … but massacred, hanged, burned and crucified with a headlong fury.'

Tacitus, writing about the destruction of London by the Iceni

A BRITISH HEROINE

Embodiment of British resistance in AD 61, Boudicca rouses the Iceni from her chariot. This 19th-century bronze sculpture on London's Victoria Embankment shows a queen who looks perhaps more Greek than British.

A SPEECH FOR THE TROOPS

Women leaders were evidently not unusual in Britain. Boudicca is said to have visited the tribes with her daughters, rousing them with fiery speeches such as those imagined by the Roman Tacitus. **'It is not as a woman descended from noble ancestors, but as one of the people that I am avenging lost freedom ... heaven is on the side of a righteous vengeance.'**

VESTIGE OF CLAUDIUS' TEMPLE
Colchester Castle's Norman keep was built directly on the foundation of the Roman temple, destroyed by the Iceni. Remnants of the temple can still be seen.

or the attractions of the place, were cut off by the enemy.' Bodies were flung into the Thames, and the Roman town burned. So did St Albans (Verulamium). In the blood-letting and looting, Tacitus says 70,000 'citizens and allies' perished.

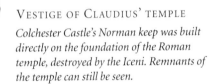

The Romans regrouped, their commander gathering an army of 10,000 men including the 14th Legion and units of the 20th, as well as auxiliaries. The 2nd Legion failed to arrive from the west as ordered, and for that its commander was obliged to commit suicide, but his judgement (or cowardice) had the effect of holding back the Silures and other western tribes from joining the general mayhem. This was just as well since Roman sources put Boudicca's army at 200,000-strong, lusting for more blood, more loot, more vengeance.

DEFEAT AND PUNISHMENT

THE ROMANS FACED the British army somewhere in the Midlands. Paulinus chose the battleground, deploying his troops on a slope with dense woodland to protect their backs, infantry in the centre, cavalry on the wings. The British thronged the ground in front of them, too many to count. Their baggage wagons drawn up behind the fighting men were packed with wives and children, cheering as spectators. A mass of Celtic warriors attacked in traditional fashion, infantry rushing forward with swords, chariots hurtling onwards at the gallop into solid ranks of Roman troops steady behind their shields.

The Romans waited, then hurled a deadly hail of javelins, causing heavy losses and confusion.

Roman infantry then advanced in tight wedge-formation, hacking and shoving their way through the struggling British, while the cavalry charged in from the flanks. The British were forced back into their own baggage-train, but the Roman cavalry killed or maimed so many horses that few could escape, and there was terrible slaughter of men, women and children. Tacitus says 80,000 British were killed, for the loss of only 400 Romans. Boudicca fled but died soon afterwards, either from illness or after taking poison to avoid capture.

ROMAN STOCKADE

The reconstructed gateway of The Lunts, a Roman fort at Baginton, Warwickshire.

Harsh punishment followed failed revolt. Paulinus laid waste British settlements as a grim and final warning. Iceni fugitives were harried as they fled, throwing away the loot they had taken during their sacking of the Roman settlements. Only loyal allies were spared fire and sword. Hungry British, their fields unsown or blackened by fire, had little stomach for more war although a few small roving bands took to the woods, still ready to resist.

Further misery was in part averted when a new Roman procurator arrived to replace Decianus Catus, the overbearing official whose harshness had enraged the Iceni. The province's new financial master, Julius Classicianus, understood that tax revenues would not recover unless the British were given the chance to rebuild. So he offered the hand of friendship, firmly but more gently.

While Romans settled to rebuild a prosperous southern province, the army still had much work to do. The south-west beyond Exeter had to be brought under control so that its tin mines might be exploited, and this meant quelling local chieftains who held out in small coastal forts. There was also unfinished business in the highlands of the west and north. Rome had to complete the conquest of Wales and in the north the legions' main task was to stop further trouble from powerful tribes like the Brigantes and to settle a 'final frontier' between Roman Britain and wild Caledonia beyond.

Over the next 50 years, the new province of Britannia was established and grew both peaceful and prosperous. Many British people became, if not Romans, then comfortable with Roman ways. Resistance was replaced by acceptance.

51

ROMANIZING BRITAIN

'Our national dress came into favour and the toga was everywhere to be seen. And so the British were gradually led on to the amenities that make vice agreeable – arcades, baths and sumptuous banquets.'

Tacitus, Agricola

BOUDICCA'S REBELLION failed to halt the legions' onward march; nor did it steady the pace of Romanization in Britain. With Caratacus in Rome and Boudicca dead, no new charismatic leaders arose to challenge Roman occupation in the islands. Client-rulers like Cogidubnus, in his elegant palace at Fishbourne, lived like Romans and happily received the rewards of this new civilization. Compromise was in the air, both sides choosing it in preference to further war. Roman feelers also reached up to the far north, to Caledonia, but the practical invaders decided this mountainous region was simply not rich enough to justify the effort of conquest. They drew a line.

Instead, steady expansion of Roman control continued from Dover in the south to Newcastle in the north. There were Roman forts in Wales, Roman roads crossing Northumbrian hills, and a great wall named in honour of the Emperor Hadrian to mark Roman Britain's northern frontier with Caledonia. Although Roman legions ventured north of the wall, they never established command over tribes living in what is now Scotland.

By AD 130 the military work was done. Much of Britain had settled to being 'Roman'. Its people lived in towns built on the Roman model, paid their taxes, visited the bathhouse, worshipped Roman gods alongside their old Celtic deities, and even learned to write. Marching soldiers, builders, lawmakers and merchants had created a new Britain, one that would last for the next 300 years.

ADOPTING ROMAN STYLE

A man and boy shown on a tombstone, wearing formal Roman dress. The man sports a toga, the child a tunic and cape fastened by brooches on the shoulders. Romanized Britons also adopted such fashions.

SOLDIERS' GOD

A marble head of Mithras, Persian god of light, whose stringent cult demanding honesty, purity and courage was favoured by Roman soldiers.

GUARDING THE WALL

Chesters Roman Fort in Northumberland seen from the north. This was one of the Roman fortified stations marking the line of Hadrian's Wall.

ON THE MARCH

Marching legionaries wore full armour, with helmets strapped to their right shoulders. On the left shoulder, each soldier rested a cross-barred pole for carrying his kit – food dish, cooking pot, clothes in a leather bag, and rations in the form of wheat-flour biscuits, bacon, cheese and sour wine.

THE ROMAN SOLDIER

MEDICAL KIT

Every soldier in the Roman army had the best of medical attention. The army's own doctors carried instruments, like those in this kit, for surgery. Mostly amputation, it was carried out with some skill but without painkillers, other than copious draughts of wine.

THE ROMAN ARMY was the ancient world's most disciplined and efficient killing machine. At its core was the legion: well-armed, well-armoured and Roman citizens to a man. Forming the assault troops for the invasion, the legions also garrisoned forts, built bridges and laid down roads.

The legion's basic unit was the century: 80 men, in ten sections of eight, commanded by a centurion. Each eight-man section shared a goatskin tent. Six centuries formed a cohort, and ten cohorts made up a legion. A legion's fighting complement comprised about 5,000 infantry with 120 cavalry troopers as scouts, orderlies and despatch riders. Among its many specialists the legion included: master builder, surveyor, catapult maker, arrow maker, boat builder, medical officer (usually a Greek), as well as priests and soothsayers.

Legions had the support of auxiliary infantry and cavalry, recruited from local tribes and other parts of the Empire, and these auxiliaries – more expendable than citizen legionaries – were usually first into the fray. Men joined the army from all parts of the Empire. Most of those serving in Britain came from what are now Holland, Belgium, France and Spain, with a small percentage from Italy. But others were from further afield: archers from Syria and cavalrymen from the Balkans.

ARMOURED FOR BATTLE

Recreation of Roman legionary troopers. Two (right and centre) wear the armour called lorica segmentata, *made from metal strips strapped together. The centurion on the left wears* lorica hamata, *or chain mail. The troopers hold* pila *(javelins) and* scuta *(curved shields).*

MOVING CAMP

A trumpet call roused soldiers to take down tents; at a second call they loaded the baggage animals and packed their own kit. The third call brought stragglers hurrying. An officer asked: 'Are you ready?' and the soldiers replied three times in unison: 'We are ready.' The march began with auxiliaries and archers leading the way, followed by legionaries and cavalry, artillery, sacred emblems and baggage train. A Roman army on the move was an awesome sight: legionaries marching six abreast behind their eagle and other standards, thousands of iron-shod boots tramping in unison up to 50 kilometres (30 miles) a day.

A legion and its auxiliary attachments were commanded by a senator. Under him were young military tribunes, all on short-service commissions before taking up public office.

Legionary soldiers did four months of basic training. During this they drilled wearing heavy backpacks and had two daily sessions of weapons training, using weighted weapons to develop muscle. Forced marches of 30 to 50 kilometres (20 to 30 miles) were common. Putting up practice camps developed skills in tree-felling, ditch-digging and rampart-raising. Every legionary had to be able to swim, cook and build. Not only had he to march with his weapons – sword and javelin – but also with his tools – spade, pick, saw and basket for shifting soil.

Roman legionaries wore armour of metal and leather, metal helmets and leather boots. They were experts with sword and dagger, spear and the javelin (*pilum*) which, when thrown, had great penetrating power. The curved shield (*scutum*), overlapped with others, could form the *testudo*, or tortoise, formation. Auxiliary troops had a less versatile, flat, oval shield and usually wore less armour.

CENTURION'S HELMET
This helmet, embossed with the eagle motif, belonged to a centurion. It had cheek-guards and a visor to protect the fore-head and eyes.

55

TO THE HIGHLANDS

STANDING STONES

A Roman stone wall still standing at the great Brigantian hill fort of Stanwick, North Yorkshire, the probable site of Venutius' last battle against the Romans.

PETILLIUS CERIALIS, former commander of the 9th Legion, returned to Roman Britain as governor in AD 71. Tasked with reorganizing an army that had 'gone soft' and was reluctant to fight, he set off for the north, taking on the Brigantes and defeating Venutius.

Conquest of the highlands of Wales and Scotland returned to the top of the military agenda during the governorships of two more formidable soldiers – Julius Frontinus (AD 74–78) and Julius Agricola (AD 78–84).

SCOTTISH SILVER

A hoard of 3rd-century Roman silver coins, found in a jar from Falkirk.

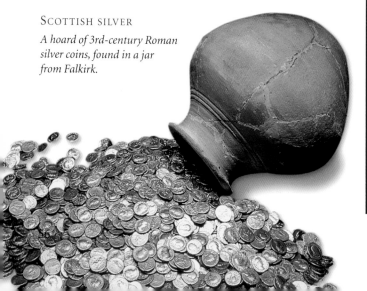

Agricola, former commander of the 20th Legion, campaigned to isolate the Celts of the Welsh highlands as three of Britain's four legions were stationed along the frontier zone: at Caerleon, Wroxeter and Chester. Even so, it took 13 campaigns to subdue the Celts of Wales, though the hills remained no-go areas. Eventually, the fierce Silures left their hill-fort capital to found the *civitas* (Roman settlement) of Caerwent in Monmouthshire. This was a privilege, granted by the Romans only to trusted tribes.

With the 20th and 9th legions, Agricola then turned north. By summer AD 81 he was in Scotland (Caledonia) on the banks of the Forth and Clyde rivers. In AD 83 the legions pushed further north into the mountains and glens, building forts as they went. Attacking at night, the 'barbarians' (called Picts or 'painted peoples' by the Romans) came close to scattering the 9th Legion before relief columns came to the rescue. In AD 84, a battle was fought at a site the Romans called Mons Graupius – possibly Bennachie in Aberdeenshire. The Caledonian leader, named as Calgacus, headed an army of around 30,000 that may well have outnumbered Agricola's.

WORDS OF DEFIANCE

Tacitus reports Calgacus' stirring words of British unity, reminding his followers that Romans had always profited from Celtic discord. It was time to stand and fight together. **'You Caledonians have never been slaves ...** there is no retreat by land and not even the sea offers escape because of the Roman ship ... **There are no more peoples behind us ...** There is nothing but rocks and waves ... **let us show what heroes Caledonia has in her bosom.'**

ANTONINE WALL

A section of turf rampart at Seabegs Wood, Bonnybridge, Stirlingshire. Roman soldiers boasted of their wall-building speed. Stone slabs at Duntocher on the Antonine Wall tell us that 'for Emperor Antoninus Augustus Pius, father of his country, the 2nd Legion built this for 3,271 feet [997 metres].'

The Celts threw in their chariots ahead of the mass of warriors, the Romans responding with a steady infantry advance led by their commander on foot. Roman cavalry scattered the chariots while the infantry slogged it out, and when the British charged downhill, more Roman horsemen rode in to encircle them.

Despite Agricola's victory, the Romans never managed to quell the Caledonian tribes. Skirmishing continued until, ruling out conquest of their territory, Emperor Hadrian fortified the northern frontier with the wall that bears his name. In AD 139–40, the Antonine Wall – named in honour of Emperor Antoninus Pius – was added as a northern defensive line between the Forth and the Clyde, but the effective frontier remained Hadrian's Wall. Beyond that, the Caledonians were left to themselves.

IN THE WILDERNESS

Traprain Law in Lothian, hill-fort capital of the Votadini tribe. Roman historians describe the hill people as wild, naked (with tattooed skins) and unshod. The Votadini later became trusted allies of Rome.

'Some 10,000 of the foe had fallen; our losses were 360.'

Tacitus, on Agricola's victory at Mons Graupius

HADRIAN'S WALL

'... present 296; from these: sick 15, wounded 6, suffering from inflammation of the eyes 10; total 31; fit for active service 265.'

Roman record-keeping details the fitness for duty of the First Cohort of Tungrians guarding Hadrian's Wall

TRIUMPH OF PERSISTENCE
Long stretches of Hadrian's Wall still rise and fall along ledges of crags and rocky sills – an impressive monument to the greatest civil-engineering project undertaken in Britain before the Industrial Revolution.

STANDING CHILLED ON a windswept Northumbrian hillside, a Roman soldier might wonder why he was patrolling such a remote and unpromising – if ruggedly beautiful – corner of the Empire. To be told his next task was to build a wall can hardly have cheered the Roman soldier. Yet build it he did, working alongside hundreds of his comrades. Hadrian's Wall was the greatest construction feat in Britain since Stonehenge. Lonely and often deserted today (away from the visitor centres), the wall was

once alive with people, civilians as well as soldiers. It remains the most famous of all Roman monuments in Britain.

A chain of forts along the Stanegate, a military road running east-west across the Tyne-Solway isthmus, formed a border – undefined and disputed – until Emperor Hadrian came to Britain in AD 122. The forts of Vindolanda and Carvoran formed part of this earlier wall, but were later amalgamated into Hadrian's Wall. Constant skirmishes with 'hostiles'

convinced Hadrian it was time for permanent damage limitation. He ordered a wall to be built from the Tyne estuary to the Solway Firth, a distance of 117 kilometres (73 miles), or 79 Roman miles. The wall was built not by slave labour but by legionaries, the elite troops of the Roman army who were as skilled in civil engineering as they were in fighting.

The plan looked daunting: a stone wall 3 metres (10 feet) wide and 5 metres (16 feet) high, with a ditch 4 metres (13 feet) deep in front. In fact the scheme was too ambitious, and specifications changed during construction. The height was reduced to 2 metres (7 feet) and the western end was finished as a turf wall with a timber palisade. The army took just seven years to build Hadrian's Wall, shifting 765,000 cubic metres (27 million cubic feet) – some 3.7 million tonnes – of locally quarried stone, carried and carted by soldiers and their conscripted labour.

Hadrian's Wall has withstood 1,600 years of pillage and decay. After the last Romans left in about AD 410, the wall became a ready source of dressed stone for building farms, towns, churches and roads.

SECOND STAGE
FORTIFICATION
Housesteads, one of 16 forts on Hadrian's Wall, was added after the legionaries had finished the initial construction.

GAMING BOARD
A gaming board, dice and counters found at Corbridge on Hadrian's Wall. People may have played games like draughts with similar counters.

LIVING ON THE EDGE

Military records found at the Roman fort of Vindolanda, near what is now Chesterholm in Northumberland, and dating from around AD 105, show incoming provisions of barley, garlic, vinegar, salt, fish sauce (a must on Roman dinner tables) and pork fat. Wine and local beer were popular. A delivery of 663 litres (146 gallons) on one June day was followed by another two days later. Wall-guarding was thirsty work! But winters were bleak. A plaintive letter, also from Chesterholm, tells the reader, **'I have sent you ... socks ... two pairs of sandals ... and two pairs of underpants.'** Roman soldiers soon found they needed to adapt their dress to the colder British weather.

CIVILIZED LIFE

'In their manners and internal policy the colonies formed a perfect representation of their great parent'.

Edward Gibbon, The Decline and Fall of the Roman Empire

THE ROMANS INTRODUCED the idea of planned towns to Britain. The Celts were not the uncivilized barbarians that many Romans thought them, yet no British Celt had so far dreamed of building a town like Roman London, or of relaxing in stone-columned splendour beside a public pool like the one at Bath. That was before the Romans came.

The Romans transformed the landscape by adding roads, country houses and farms, but above all they changed the face of Britain by sprinkling it with towns that had noisy streets, busy shops, workshops, government offices and army garrisons. Britons took to city sophistication enthusiastically. They began to wear Roman clothes and went to the bathhouse, the games and the theatre – and enjoyed the fun. They drank wine, which made a change from beer, and they had new gods to worship alongside those they had always known. 'Abroad' had come to Britain in a big way. It was a heady experience.

This astonishing change happened with surprising speed – southern Britain was 'Romanized' while the north was still echoing to the march of the legions. By the time Boudicca's Iceni warriors swept down on Colchester (18 years after the Roman invasion), the town already had a civic hall, theatre, temple with Roman statues, and shops selling pottery imported from Gaul. London was becoming 'an important centre for businessmen and merchandise,' says Tacitus, and by AD 80 it boasted the governor's palace and an impressive forum and basilica (town hall and court of justice).

There was no real contest between the old and new, though the old Celtic ways and beliefs survived in some parts of Britain. Romanization – much like Americanization in many parts of the world today – was unstoppable.

ROMAN BATH

Bath was unique as a spa resort among Roman-British towns. It was cosmopolitan, and people seeking cures came to its baths from all over Europe. The Romans channelled the thermal spring water into a huge lead-lined bath, and built a bath complex around it.

AT THE RACES

A mosaic showing a chariot race, found at Horkstow Villa in Lincolnshire, and dating from around AD 340.

A FINE LIFE

Lullingstone Villa in Kent, a reconstruction of the farmstead as it looked about AD 380, after a small corner had been converted to a Christian chapel. Boasting fine mosaics, this villa may have been used primarily as a holiday home.

GOVERNMENT AND CITIZENSHIP

THE ROMANS BELIEVED in letting subject people govern themselves. By granting self-government to British tribes, they passed responsibility for civilized government (law enforcement, tax collecting, civic affairs) to local leaders.

Province Britannia had a governor, a high-ranking Roman usually from an army background. The early governors were briefed, like Agricola in the north, to extend the Empire and mark the new frontier. Later governors had to make sure that Roman Britain was peaceful and prosperous and – as the years passed – were required to organize defence against threats from new invaders.

'In place of a distaste for the Latin language came a passion to command it.'

Tacitus, on how Agricola trained the sons of British chiefs

At the governor's side was a procurator, who was in charge of finance and taxation. These were the chief executives. From their offices, directives passed down to the councils at lower levels: the *coloniae* (army veterans), the *municipia* (towns) and *civitates* (tribal territories). Tribal councils overseeing large regions had up to 100 members, and from these four magistrates were chosen (two senior, two junior). One pair administered civil law, including crime. The other two ran everyday affairs in their region – from road-repair to the construction of new public buildings.

Roman law was put in force after the conquest. Romans had a high regard for lawyers: they were in great demand, charged hefty fees and rose to high political office. Town magistrates were elected by the citizens and campaigns were often lively – graffiti-covered walls have been found extolling the merits or condemning the vices of various candidates. Common among the ruins of Pompeii in Italy, such graffiti must also have been plastered all over buildings in Roman Britain.

THE TAX MAN

Reconstructed tombstone of Julius Classicianus, 1st-century procurator of Roman Britain. Pieces of the original, found in London's Trinity Square, had been used to build a bastion of the city walls. The inscription reads 'To the spirits of the departed [and] of Gaius Julius Alpinus Classicianus, son of Gaius, of the Fabian voting tribe … Julia Pacata I [Indiana], daughter of Indus, his wife, had this built.'

WAX MAIL

A wax tablet on which official business could be written, enclosed and sealed. The wax could be smoothed over for reuse.

CAMPAIGNING GOVERNORS OF ROMAN BRITAIN

The complete list of Roman governors of Britain is as yet still hazy, but the names and dates of the first 11 post-invasion governors are:

43–47	Aulus Plautius
47–52	Publius Ostorius Scapula
52–57	Aulus Didius Gallus
57–58	Quintus Veranius
58–61	Gaius Suetonius Paulinus
61/62–63	Publius Petronius Turpilianus
63–69	Marcus Trebellius Maximus
69–71	Marcus Vettius Bolanus
71–73/74	Quintus Petillius Cerialis
73/74–77/78	Sextus Julius Frontinus
77/78–83/84	Gnaeus Julius Agricola

Legionary soldiers were proud of being Roman citizens. Britons could also become Roman citizens, through army service or civic virtue – for example, by being a trustworthy ally or a stern but honest dispenser of justice. From Silchester we know of a Celt from the Tammonii clan who – calling himself Saenius Tammonus – had become a magistrate (Romans had three names, so this man would have had a first name too). His son, to sound even more Roman, called himself T. Tammonus Vitalis. A new three-part Roman family name (forename, clan name, surname) had been created from a Celtic one in a generation.

WEIGHING THE GOODS

A bronze steelyard, with lead weight, as used by traders and shopkeepers. Goods were hung from the hooks, and weighed by sliding the weight along the graduated arm.

63

TRADE AND INDUSTRY

TOWN LIFE LED TO a business boom as wealthier Britons acquired a taste for the Roman lifestyle. Their new Italian-design houses needed building and furnishing materials; their tables called for fine foods and wines; their bodies looked better in expensive Roman styling. Even so, while the upper crust lived in elegant, centrally heated town houses, most people stayed put in their simple wooden homes. Many were shopkeepers or craftsmen, trading from front rooms open to the street to display their goods.

Trading success can be judged by London's rapid growth, thrusting its way to become the province's business centre and capital by the AD 80s. Into the city sailed shiploads of pottery, notably the glossy red Samian ware much in demand by the fashion-conscious. Local potteries also developed, for example in the New Forest area and around Oxford. Wine – running a close second to pottery as Britain's most valued import – was shipped in on large sailing vessels carrying hundreds of amphorae (jars) as well as glassware from Gaul and Italy. From London and other ports, barges carried goods around the coast and along rivers, trading into towns such as Chester and York by water rather than road. Roads were primarily military routes, though slow-moving ox-wagons and pack-horses used them too.

Delicacies, especially olive oil, were mostly imported. However, Roman Britain did become increasingly self-sufficient, exporting its prized oysters (and the already famous

thick cloak, the *birrus Britannicus*), together with corn, iron, copper, tin, silver and gold.

Mining became a key activity in Britain's mineral-rich land. Lead from the Mendips, Peak District and North Wales was mixed with tin from Cornwall to make pewter. Pewter tableware looked good and, cheaper than silver, found a ready market. Marble had to be imported but local stone was used for building, and even to make tables and couches – Romans liked stone furniture!

POPULAR POT

A shiny red Samian-ware pot from a 2nd-century Roman-British home. British elements in the design include curling tendrils and animal ornament.

MONEY MAKES THE WORLD GO AROUND …

Roman coins were made from gold, silver, bronze and copper. Given a fixed value by the first emperor, Augustus (27 BC–AD 14), coins were used throughout the Empire for trade.

OFF-LOADING IN LONDON

A Roman ship unloads building stone at London's Fleet River. A ship like the one shown in this artist's impression was found in the River Thames at Blackfriars. A cargo vessel is berthed to the right.

Local craftsmen turned out tools, furniture and such everyday items as cooking pots. Among the most respected specialists were blacksmiths, with their mastery of fire and melting metal. Using planes, trowels, hammers and chisels almost identical to today's hand-tools, carpenters and builders were kept busy. British craftsmen learned new skills, using stone, brick, marble and mosaic to transform their homeland into a prosperous province of the world's greatest commercial – as well as military – empire.

BLACKSMITH AT WORK

A blacksmith, pictured on a tombstone now in the Yorkshire Museum, York.

ROMAN LONDON

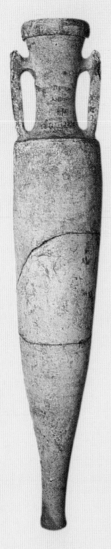

THOUGH NO PRE-ROMAN name for it has yet appeared, a British settlement may well have existed near the place where London Bridge now stands. Londinium, as the Romans knew it, did not play much of a part in Roman Britain's story until Boudicca's war-crazed warriors ravaged the small town on the River Thames. Its rebuilding was a vital part of the reconstruction of Roman Britain which the imperialists now began.

A wooden bridge across the Thames, put up by troops soon after they landed in Britain, had become the focal point of a flourishing port and trading settlement. Boudicca's warriors left this first Roman town in flames. Skulls recovered from the bed of Walbrook stream (see page 51) bear witness to the slaughter, and a layer of reddish burnt clay – uncovered by excavations in the old city's modern financial heart, around Lombard Street – carries the imprint of the raging inferno that destroyed the wooden buildings.

WHAT A SAUCE!

Large Roman jars, or amphorae, were used to carry and store olive oil, wine, fish sauce or other goods. Remains of the Romans' favourite fish sauce were in this amphora. Dating from AD 70–120, the amphora has an inscription painted on its neck in Latin claiming that 'Lucius Tertius Africanus supplies the finest fish sauce from Antibes.'

Rebuilt on a grander scale, London became the new province's centre of government and commerce. Here was the office of the procurator, Julius Classicianus, whose moderate good sense did much to soothe British wrath. He died in London and bits of his tombstone survive – one piece found in 1852, another in 1939 (see page 62). Governors of Roman Britain made London their

LONDON'S TRADE

This model of the Roman waterfront at Lower Thames Street, London, around AD 100, is based on excavations in the area. The wooden bridge joining the northern and southern halves of the city is busy with traffic moving to and from the riverside warehouses.

WALLED CITY

Parts of the old Roman wall around London have survived for almost 2,000 years, while the city itself has grown and changed around them.

headquarters and, some time before AD 100, a large and handsome palace was built (on the site of today's Cannon Street Station). London developed as a Roman city, with a forum, a basilica, bathhouses, shops, warehouses, amusements and private houses of various sizes. Although a second fire around AD 125 destroyed many wooden buildings, it did not end the city's steady expansion as a busy port and commercial centre.

Ship-borne trade boomed as timber wharves and warehouses were built along the banks of the Thames. This lay about 100 metres (109 yards) north of today's riverbank, centuries of development having shifted it southwards. Remains of several ships, including a barge laden with building stone, have been found buried in Thames mud.

London's citizens had the choice of goods from all over the Roman Empire – pottery from Gaul and Germany, and glass from Italy. Amphorae of wine came from Italy and Spain, while cheaper wine (in barrels) was shipped from Gaul. Spain supplied olive oil; the Baltic lands, amber beads; Italy and Greece, marble for building and tombstones. Jet came from Yorkshire, lead from Derbyshire, and tin from Cornwall.

Around AD 200, a wall 3 kilometres (2 miles) long was built around the city, enclosing an area of 330 acres. Probably 6 metres (20 feet) high, the wall was made from hundreds of tonnes of Kentish ragstone. Gatehouses set in the wall allowed roads to run through. The main gates were used well into medieval times, their names surviving as Bishopsgate, Aldgate, Newgate and Ludgate. Traces of the wall remain to this day.

FARMS AND VILLAS

'*… so plentiful are its harvests, so numerous are the pasturelands in which it rejoices.*'

Eumenius, Roman orator and teacher, on rural Britain
c. AD 300

As Britons copied Roman ways, more people began to lead town lives, no longer growing their own food. The new urban middle class joined the old tribal nobility in quickly acquiring a taste for Mediterranean-style dining.

Meanwhile, the huge army of legionaries and auxiliaries stationed at forts around the province also required regular rations. Farming became not only economically essential, but also profitable. Small farmers used to producing enough meat, grain and vegetables to feed their own families and near neighbours now found they could sell surplus produce for cash, by taking the road to the nearest market town.

The Romans were great improvers. Virgil, their greatest poet, had been an enthusiastic supporter of rural life, and other writers had compiled guides on good farming practice. Following Roman advice, British farmers began to try out new methods. Farmhouses themselves also changed as – over generations – simple dwellings were extended, rebuilt and once again enlarged. Furnished in Roman style, they became villas on the Italian model, country houses of wealthy townspeople and landowners. The villa had its own bathhouse, formal gardens, accommodation for family and guests, estate offices, and living quarters for farm bailiffs, servants and slaves.

Owners of large villas employed a secretary, clerks and scribes to keep records, in order to pay taxes accurately. An overseer

PLOUGHMAN AT WORK

A 2nd-century bronze statuette of a ploughman with an ox and cow, from the Roman fort at Piercebridge, County Durham.

COUNTRY VILLA

Villas were country houses on farmland. Those owned by wealthy landowners were extended into luxurious homes, as grand as their counterparts in Italy.

might be put in charge if the owner lived in town. Most of the villa workers were hired locally. Slaves belonged to the estate, like the livestock. Workers included herdsmen, ploughmen, smiths, gardeners, carpenters, wagon drivers and potters.

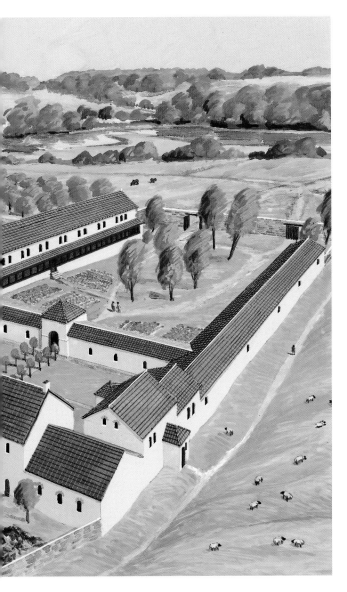

BATHHOUSE AT CHEDWORTH

Part of the bathhouse at Chedworth Villa, showing the mosaic floor of the warm room (tepidarium), *the wall flues and hypocaust pillars beneath the hot room* (caldarium).

The largest villas were great country houses built on a grand scale. Grandest of all was the palatial Fishbourne (see pages 70–71), but more usual was its Sussex neighbour, Bignor, with surrounding estates of about 3,000 acres. Even so, most villas were smaller, the centres of working farms. Larger villas often sported lavish decoration, with tastefully painted plaster walls. When the weather was chilly, British villa owners turned on the underfloor heating provided by a hypocaust hot-air system in the main rooms. Daylight indoors must have been dim, as window glass was translucent green. Oil lamps, lit at dusk, provided a soft flickering glow but little useful light, so most people retired to bed.

Grain could be threshed by hand in the large farmyard and damp corn dried in hot-air kilns. Large villas might have a walled village within the estate.

In the 4th century, many British villas were enlarged or improved. Already sizeable, Chedworth in Gloucestershire had a large new dining room installed, along with two sets of baths, hot and cold. In the 2nd century, fewer than ten British villas had mosaic floors; even modest country houses had them 200 years later.

ROMAN PORTRAIT

Wall painting from the bathhouse of a villa at Sparsholt, Hampshire, now at the Winchester City Museum.

FISHBOURNE'S MARVELS

Art in Roman Britain copied and at times surpassed that of Rome itself. Fishbourne Roman Palace was as grand as any building in Italy. Its decorations included stunning mosaics like this Cupid on a dolphin.

IN 1960, A WORKMAN digging a trench for a water main north of the West Sussex village of Fishbourne, near Chichester, unearthed a mass of ancient rubble.

Archaeologists were startled to discover that here lay the remains of a huge Roman mansion. Their excavations revealed a building that fully justifies the title 'palace', though whose home it was remains uncertain.

Covering 5.6 acres, Fishbourne would have rivalled palaces in Rome and the Roman governor's residence in London. Possibly the governor used it, or perhaps it was the home of a rich British ally of the Romans, Tiberius Claudius Cogidubnus, the region's most powerful ruler in the 1st century AD.

The original palace had some 100 rooms, most of which probably had mosaic

CHANNELLLED HEATING
A channelled hypocaust heating system built at Fishbourne Roman Palace in the 3rd century.

floors, laid by expert workers from Gaul or Italy. About a quarter of these floors survive, the largest collection of mosaic floors still in place anywhere in Britain. Most rooms opened out onto columned walkways and from the south, guests could admire terraced gardens, with hedge-lined paths, a stream, pool and fountains, fed by ceramic water pipes – and a splendid view of the sea. Most rooms also probably had painted walls and ceilings; no two rooms seem to have been the same. Tantalizingly little interior decoration survives. Fragments of moulded stucco friezes show birds with fruit in their beaks, while part of a marble head shows a child, perhaps a member of the owner's family.

Building work began at Fishbourne in the AD 60s, after the Romans had set up a wooden army camp beside the nearby harbour. The first buildings, of timber and stone, were pulled down around AD 75 and the new villa begun. More changes were made over the years, until fire destroyed the great house some time towards the end of the 3rd century, possibly while alterations were in progress. Usable material was then removed from the debris, the decision having been taken not to rebuild. Later generations carted away the stone for their own building projects, and what remained was hidden beneath pastureland. Today only part of the great building's outline can be seen following excavation. The south wing lies beneath a nearby road and houses; the north wing remains are preserved in a museum, where visitors can see the mosaics at close hand.

THE GARDENS AT FISHBOURNE

Roman gardens were regular in design with columns, statues, rows of trees, formal flower beds, hedging, paths and fountains all set out at measured intervals. Linen curtains and awnings were sometimes hung outside for added shade and interest. Most gardens had a niched shrine and some even had their own temples. Fishbourne had one of Britain's grandest Roman gardens, planted with such favourite flowers as lilies, roses, lavender, violet, myrtle and acanthus. There were also herbs (hyssop, thyme, coriander and mint) used in cooking Mediterranean-influenced dishes, and in medicines. The courtyard garden, watered by underground piping and manured with kitchen refuse, has been reconstructed following archaeological evidence, but an even larger naturally landscaped garden existed at Fishbourne, sloping in wide terraces down to the waterside nearby.

FLAVIAN MOSAIC
The Flavian mosaic, dating from the 1st century AD, lay in the centre of the north wing of the palace.

ROMAN TOWNS

'… so many are the metals of which seams run through it, so much wealth comes from its taxes, so many ports encircle it …'

Eumenius, writing of the wealth of Britain, c. AD 300

BRITAIN'S WEALTH GREW with its towns. The Romans – Britain's first town planners – had begun building Colchester within six years of the AD 43 invasion, basing it around a legionary fort set up on the Trinovantes' tribal capital, Camulodunum. This was a *colonia*, a town largely reserved for army veterans. The Romans called it a *municipium*: the town was self-governing, but everyone had to obey Roman law, administered by magistrates and town council on the Roman pattern.

Other major towns in Roman Britain followed this model: London, Lincoln, Gloucester and York. Lesser towns – known as *civitates* – maintained some degree of British tribal law and organization, and local nobles elected the magistrates. Many small towns started as squatter camps set up by traders and camp followers trailing behind the legions. Living in shanty homes outside a walled fort, they were on the spot to make rich pickings from the relatively well-off soldiery. Rough settlements like these were later regulated as *vici*, with permanent homes and shops under army supervision.

Roman-British towns were laid out with streets in a grid pattern. Liking order and neatness, the planners repeated Italy's city patterns, so that a visitor from Rome might feel at home in London's streets, even under cloudy skies. Dominating the town

centre was the forum, a large colonnaded courtyard serving as market and meeting place, where deals were done and politicians looked for votes. On one side was the basilica, the town hall and court of justice, where tribunes sat to consider cases. Offenders found guilty faced a fine, loss of property, flogging, hard labour in mines or quarries, or execution.

FOOT LIGHT

Terracotta oil lamp in the shape of a human foot, found in the Southwark district of London. Filled with olive oil and lit with a wick, such lamps shed a subdued glow.

PICTURE PAVING

Mosaic, a favourite form of decoration in Roman homes, also appeared in public places. This detail is from a mosaic pavement dating from the 2nd century. It can now be seen in Winchester City Museum.

Despite their grand buildings, Roman-British towns were small compared to those of today. London, the biggest, was the fourth largest city north of the Alps yet at 330 acres was no larger than the square mile of today's City of London.

Evidence for how many Roman Britons there were is sketchy, but some historians estimate the population by the 4th century at around 5 million – perhaps twice that of Britain at the time of the Norman Conquest in 1066.

ROMAN TOWN CENTRE

This reconstruction shows Wroxeter in Roman times. On the right is the square-shaped forum, with a covered walkway on three sides containing shops and offices, and on the fourth is the basilica or town hall.

73

ROMANS AT LEISURE

THE ROMANS WERE hardworking though sometimes severe (pointing out the merits and high moral fibre of their ancestors), but liked nothing better than to relax and have a good time.

Public baths and those for army use were the sport and fitness centres of their day. Outdoor swimming pools were rare, although there was one at Wroxeter. Even while keeping fit and clean, Romans indulged in the gambling habit that had many of them hooked. Soldiers were especially keen on dice, and people placed bets on all kinds of games, on gladiator fights and on horse and chariot races. Many towns boasted an amphitheatre or stadium and some, such as that at Caerleon, were large, seating 6,000 fans on wooden seats arranged on stone terraces. Caerleon's amphitheatre, the best preserved in Britain, is a squat oval shape measuring 76 metres by 61 metres (250 feet by 200 feet).

Open-air arenas could be used for army training, but also for games staged on religious and military festivals, and on special public holidays such as the emperor's birthday. Roman sports could be cruel and grisly; the mob was always ready to see blood spilt for its amusement, be it that of captured wild animals or human gladiators.

Trained to fight in a variety of styles, gladiators were the best-paid celebrities of the Roman entertainment world and top-flight stars earned fortunes. Killing one another was wasteful of talent, so instead the best fighters entertained crowds by slaughtering

HEAVYWEIGHT BOXER

A bronze weight in the shape of a boxer. Cauliflower ears and a pigtail (often worn by Roman boxers and wrestlers) make this a lifelike representation.

NEMESIUM SHRINE

This small shrine to Nemesis, Greek goddess of retribution, stands next to the north entrance of Chester's amphitheatre, which had room for up to 7,000 spectators.

prisoners of war or convicted criminals. Condemned men went into the arena to die in a public and ruthless execution – apart from those rare few who were lucky or skilful enough to turn the tables on their opponent.

Popular shows were provided by acrobats and jugglers, wrestlers, boxers (who, with metal gloves, gave – and took – terrible beatings), bear-baiting and mock-hunts of captive animals, such as wild boar. These 'entertainments' were a useful political tool. Every Roman governor or emperor knew the importance of keeping the people happy.

St Albans (Verulamium) still has its Roman theatre, built in the mid-2nd century. It is one of only four Roman theatres known in Britain: the others are at Canterbury, Colchester and Brough, Cumbria. Of all these, St Albans is the finest, built on classical lines to replace an earlier theatre burned down in AD 155. Horseshoe-shaped tiers of seats view the stone stage, which had a backdrop of columns. Here actors appeared in plays (often bawdy comedies) and pantomimes, or performed songs and recitations. Romans enjoyed the theatre, though their dramas were less religious, less serious (and less good) than those of the Greeks. Some actors' masks made of clay or ivory have also survived.

ACTOR'S MASK
Roman plays often had complicated plots but the character types could be identified by their masks, making it easier to work out who was who.

PREMIER PLAYHOUSE
The theatre at St Albans (Verulamium) is the best-preserved Roman theatre in Britain. Built after a fire had destroyed much of the town, and later enlarged, it was almost circular.

75

ROMAN BATHS

Soldiers based at Wroxeter's legionary garrison could relax off-duty in the town baths. This view of the site shows the bath complex in the foreground with the exercise hall beyond.

> *'Picture to yourself the assortment of sounds which are obnoxious ... when your strenuous gentleman is exercising himself.'*
>
> Seneca, 1st century AD, on living next door to the baths

CELTS WERE NOTED FOR THEIR cleanliness, but taking a bath meant far more than hygiene to Romans. Social life centred on the bathhouse, a large and grand complex serving as health and social club, sauna, sports club and wine bar. It was a place to relax, take a hot or cold water plunge, and unwind after the rigours of the day – or even before the rigours had begun.

Every town had a bath complex; so did roadside inns and all the best private houses. Some legionary fortresses had baths of magnificent proportions. Among these were the fortress baths at Caerleon in Wales, which were originally 110 metres (330 feet) long, rivalling a medieval cathedral. The main outdoor swimming pool, supplied with water through lead pipes, was 41 metres (135 feet) long and held 365,000 litres (80,300 gallons). The bathing complex, including the exercise hall, was under cover.

Bathing was a pleasant ritual. Having undressed in the changing room, a bather walked through a sequence of hot, warm and cold rooms, both dry and wet. Slaves were on hand to rub oil into the bather's body, letting it seep into pores opened by

THE BATHS AT BATH

Aquae Sulis was a spa town prospering from the thermal spring that flowed with the sacred healing waters of Sulis (a Celtic deity twinned by Romans with their goddess Minerva). Building a temple on the spot held sacred by Celts for hundreds of years, the Romans channelled the waters into a huge lead-lined bath, adding a bath complex and exercise hall. People came from far and wide to take the plunge, seeking energy renewal and cures. Spirits that could heal might also mar or maim and Bath was a good place to lay a curse on an enemy, by writing backwards. One lead tablet from the reservoir fed by the sacred spring carries the grim threat: **'May he who carried off Vilbia from me become liquid as the water.'** Several culprits are then named, both male and female, perhaps to extract maximum value from the curse invocation.

IN HOT WATER

Steaming waters from the thermal spring at Bath flowed through brick-channelled pipes into the magnificent Roman swimming pool. An overflow system, still working, carried surplus water to the River Avon.

the steamy warmth. Then, in the hottest rooms, oil, sweat and dirt were all removed with a curved metal scraper or strigil. Rinsing in a warm-water bath was followed by a bracing cold plunge to close the pores once more. A massage might ease aching muscles, or soothe away stress. The leisurely process, enjoyed by men and women (though normally separately), was a social occasion allowing ample time for gossip, exchanging news and views, placing bets and planning future enterprises.

Of all Roman-British towns, the most bath-conscious was Bath (Aquae Sulis) where people arrived – as they still do today – to take the waters. Grander than most Celtic-Roman temples, Bath's bathhouse was a full-scale classical building housing a gilded statue of Minerva that glowed in the light of an eternal flame.

POOL PLAYING

Bathhouses included an exercise hall, the palaes-tra, *which had space for people to wrestle, lift weights, stroll and chat, buy snacks from food and drink vendors, or lose their money gambling.*

CELTIC GORGON

This sculpted head glared out from the temple at Bath. It portrayed a Roman gorgon as a barbarian Celt, embodying the spirit of the goddess Sulis Minerva.

FOOD AND FASHION

RICH ROMANIZED BRITONS lived in some style and comfort at home. Men opting for Roman fashion wore a simply cut tunic that doubled as a nightshirt. When on official business, they draped themselves in a toga (an oval or semicircle of woollen cloth), worn with high shoes called *calcei*, but otherwise put on a long over-tunic held in by a belt or girdle and, in cold weather, a cloak.

A woman with servants to help her dress had plenty of time to spend on her appearance. She peered at her face in a mirror of polished bronze, as her hair was dressed with a bone comb. The hairstyle was likely to be elaborate, often involving hairpieces and wigs, but her skincare routine harboured unknown hazards. White lead, among other ingredients such as ochre, chalk and charcoal, was ground in oils to make cosmetic pastes. Dress was basically a layered look – an ankle-length tunic worn beneath a shorter top tunic or toga-style drape – and sandals the footwear. The colour of a woman's dress would denote her rank in society, as would the jewellery she wore. A noble lady (patrician) could wear a diadem on her head; a humbler woman

ELEGANT TOPKNOT

Ornate plaiting and curling of hair was fashionable among wealthy women eager to copy styles popular in Rome. This style dates from the time of Roman expansion in Britain (AD 69–100).

A ROMAN KITCHEN

A Roman kitchen reconstructed at the Verulamium Museum, St Albans, gives an idea of the wide range of storage jars used for cookery ingredients.

could not. Statues and paintings show a variety of fashions over the centuries, with hairstyles ranging from the severely straight to waves and curls, sometimes produced with the aid of hot tongs. A cemetery at York yielded a woman's reddish-brown bun, held in place by long hair pins.

Mealtimes were leisurely. Wealthy Roman Britons had slaves who did the cooking –

> *'By the true Bacchus I know you not, he smells of nectar, you smell of goat.'*
>
> *The wine-loving Emperor Julianus (c. AD 283), giving his opinion of Celtic beer*

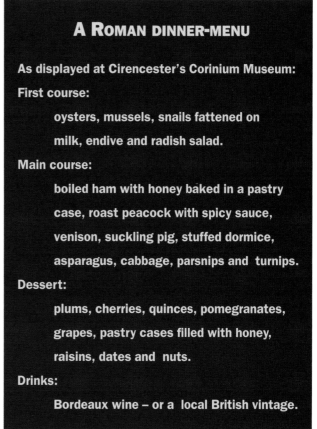

A ROMAN DINNER-MENU

As displayed at Cirencester's Corinium Museum:

First course:

oysters, mussels, snails fattened on milk, endive and radish salad.

Main course:

boiled ham with honey baked in a pastry case, roast peacock with spicy sauce, venison, suckling pig, stuffed dormice, asparagus, cabbage, parsnips and turnips.

Dessert:

plums, cherries, quinces, pomegranates, grapes, pastry cases filled with honey, raisins, dates and nuts.

Drinks:

Bordeaux wine – or a local British vintage.

supervised in the kitchen by the lady of the house – over charcoal embers burning on a raised stone hearth. Bread was baked in a charcoal or wood-fuelled oven. Most kitchen utensils would be recognizable today, although available only in iron, wood or pottery. Red Samian pottery from Gaul was commonly used for everyday tableware but on special occasions, silver or pewter dishes were produced for serving. Diners ate with spoons and knives (guests having brought their own), but no forks. Choice finger-food morsels were therefore on every menu, within easy-picking reach of diners reclining on couches at low tables.

The main meal – taken in the evening – was liberally washed down by well-to-do families with Italian, Spanish or Gaulish wines that were far more refreshing to the taste buds than the vinegary 'plonk' swilled by thirsty soldiers. Unimpressed Britons still enjoyed their beer brewed from barley, or mead made from fermented honey and water.

WELSH GEM

A jewellery piece decorated with cornelians, blue paste and bordered with filigree. It was found at Rhayader in Wales.

FAMILY LIFE

Prudent slaves could save enough from perks to buy their freedom, or might be set free by their masters as a thank you for good service.

Romanized families – those who could pay servants or buy slaves to look after them – lived like Romans, for whom family life anchored society. A man was master in his own household and women (though with fewer legal rights) were often put on a pedestal and expected to embody all the noblest Roman virtues. Many girls married young (at 14 or 15), and while a few women stayed single, they usually found it hard economically and socially. Weddings – sometimes arranged between families, but just as often the result of free choice – were celebrated with customs still familiar today (such as carrying the bride

WHERE THE FAMILY ATE

A 1st-century Roman dining room reconstructed at the Museum of London, using objects discovered on city sites. Household items had to be imported at first, until local industries began making them.

IN SPITE OF THE MOMENTOUS changes that had taken place in their land, for most Britons daily life went on much as it had for their Celtic ancestors. Houses were simple and undecorated, clothes made from homespun wool, and meals rather repetitive: bread and porridge, with vegetable stews and a little meat when available. Children played in fields and woods, though wary of roaming wild boar or wolves. They also helped adults keep the family fed and warm. Adults worked hard, either for themselves or for a master. Most slaves, household or estate, tended to live on the property to which they were bound.

Some slaves lived as part of – but not one of – the family. Others ran businesses for their masters and a few reached the top of the civil service or local government.

ROMAN PURSE

Romans loved to shop, and when Roman Britons went on a spending spree they would carry money in a wrist purse.

80

over the threshold and wearing a wedding ring on the third finger of the left hand). At funerals, traditional formalities were observed. Not only were the dead person's merits remembered, but the ancestral virtues of family and nation.

Children whose parents wanted them educated – and could afford it – were taught to read and write, often by a literate slave. Only boys were sent to school; girls were taught at home, with an emphasis on domestic skills. But the vast majority of children in Roman Britain were educated by learning the skills of their parents or close relatives.

Spare time at home was filled with reading, writing letters or playing board games much like draughts and chess, using bone or pottery playing pieces. People sang popular and traditional songs, playing the lyre and *cithera*, an 11- or 12-stringed triangular instrument.

With town houses came formal gardens – for relaxation, exercise, and home-grown produce. Britain's first gardeners may well have been Romans – they certainly introduced the formal, planned type of garden complete with ponds, fountains, and neatly laid out beds for herbs, fruit, vegetables and flowers. Hundreds of new plant species were first dug into British soil by green-fingered Romans. They included many herbs – parsley, sage, lovage, thyme, rosemary, fennel – as well as perhaps 400 more familiar plants including cherries, grapes, figs, mulberries, radishes, peas, broad beans and celery – providing Britons with a healthier, more varied diet.

PEACE AND TRANQUILLITY
Courtyard garden of a Roman town house, recreated at the Corinium Museum, Cirencester.

FAMILY FRIEZE
Carving from the tomb of M. Cornelius Statius (now in the Louvre Museum, Paris), showing a family scene with parents and children.

IN THEIR OWN WORDS: VINDOLANDA

MUCH OF THE 'HUMAN INTEREST' evidence of Roman Britain comes from inscriptions written on tombstones, altars and memorials, from letters and from documents. For example, we know of a wine merchant named Lunaris who travelled between York and Bordeaux, where he dedicated an altar in thanks for his safe journey. We know also of Regina, the British wife of a trader named Barates from the Levant (Lebanon/Syria), whose tombstone was found at South Shields, Tyne and Wear. Graffiti scrawled on walls or on wet clay by workers tells its own story (in Latin, the only written language of Roman Britain): 'Clementinus made this box-tile … I smashed 51 …'.

Most appealing of all are the documents discovered at Vindolanda (modern Chesterholm in Northumberland) – a Roman fort and civilian settlement established along the Stanegate Road, some 20 years before Hadrian's Wall was built. Here are the remains of buildings (houses and shops, a bathhouse and rest-house for travellers), as well as a modern reconstruction of the turf wall and wooden fence, to give an idea of what the fortifications were like.

The Vindolanda writing tablets, now in the British Museum, are slivers of thin wood, rather like veneer postcards, on which the users wrote in ink with a reed pen. Fourteen pens were discovered in one room, probably the local army office. Thrown away on rubbish tips between AD 80 and 130, the tablets have survived for centuries owing to the unusual moist chemistry of the soil in which they lay for almost 1,900 years.

The Vindolanda tablets were penned by a variety of authors – army officers, ordinary soldiers, traders, women, slaves. Among them are official reports, lists of food wanted by the army, letters from one businessman to another, letters home, an invitation to a friend. Tablet 344 is a draft letter of complaint from a person anxious to plead his innocence of some offence. He writes, possibly to the governor himself, 'as befits an honest man I

ROMAN INKPOT

A Roman inkpot with writing instruments, as used by the Vindolanda writers and others in Roman Britain. Ink was made from carbon, gum arabic and water.

'Give my greetings to your Cerialis. My Aelius and my little son send him [?] their greetings … Farewell, sister, my dearest soul, as I hope to prosper.'

Letter to Sulpicia Lepidina, wife of Flavius Cerialis, from Claudia Severa

WORDS ON WOOD

This tablet has a line from Virgil's Aeneid scribbled on it; the writer used the back of a tablet on which a private letter had been started but left unfinished.

implore your majesty not to allow me, an innocent man, to be beaten with rods.' Another tablet (233) is from Flavius Cerialis to 'his Brocchus': 'If you love me brother, I ask that you send me some hunting nets … you should repair the pieces very strongly …'. The Vindolanda letters are vivid proof that Roman Britain had a literate culture – one tablet quotes a line from the great Roman epic, the *Aeneid* – and that written letters and notes were used by ordinary people for everyday business. The letter from Claudia Severa, wife of Aelius Brocchus, to Sulpicia Lepidina is a rare example of a birthday invitation, and one of the earliest-known examples of handwriting in Latin by a woman.

BIRTHDAY INVITATION

'Make sure you come, to make the day more enjoyable for me,' says a birthday invitation from Claudia Severa to her friend Sulpicia Lepidina, from the Roman fort at Vindolanda.

STANEGATE ROAD

This reconstruction shows the fort established on the Stanegate Road in Northumberland. A timber fort was replaced by a stone fort when Hadrian's Wall was constructed.

RELIGION AND FESTIVALS

'Let him who stole it [a linen cloth] not have rest until he brings the aforesaid thing to the aforesaid temple.'

A woman named Saturnina appealing to the god Mercury to curse a thief; written on a lead tablet that was found in Gloucestershire

STONE-FACED DEITY

A goddess in stone from Chedworth Villa in Gloucestershire. Images of gods played an important part in Celtic-Roman religion.

THE SUPERSTITIOUS ROMANS picked up a collection of gods from the people they conquered – perhaps to avoid upsetting any alien spirits – and so happily took on board many Celtic beliefs. Pre-Roman Britons celebrated four great seasonal festivals. At the end of October came Samain, a night when magic burst loose into the world. It marked the turn of the year, when farm animals were slaughtered before winter. Imbolc heralded the start of lambing, in February, and Beltane in May saw the cattle sent out to graze, passing between lighted fires. Lugnasad fell at the beginning of August, as crops ripened. These old Celtic customs and traditions lingered long in Britain, well beyond the arrival of Christianity.

To most Romans, however, Jupiter was always 'the best and greatest' of their deities. Other gods and goddesses tended to swap order in the heavenly hierarchy to fit the needs of the time or person.

Families had shrines in their houses where they worshipped their god or goddess of choice, together with the household spirits: the Lares and Penates, Vesta (goddess of the domestic hearth) and Janus, two-faced guardian god of the doorway (who gave our month of January its name).

Soldiers had their own favourite gods but Mithras, Persian god of light, fitted the requirements of many tough legionaries. His men-only cult demanded absolute secrecy and a painful, frightening initiation ceremony. Soldiers were also expected to show devotion to the emperor. Emperor-worship was a powerful unifying force throughout the Empire, especially for the army: it was the emperor's image that led them into battle, and it was for the emperor that troops must be ready to die. Almost all religions were tolerated, unless they were subversive. At first Christianity was among the exceptions since it did not accept emperor-worship, but in AD 313 Emperor Constantine gave freedom of worship to Christians too.

Prominent in the Roman Empire from AD 324, Christianity had already taken hold in Britain, where evidence of its practice can be found in wall paintings at Lullingstone Villa and a mosaic from Hinton St Mary. The martyrdom of St Alban – a Roman soldier convert killed in AD 304 (traditionally at Verulamium) in place of a persecuted priest – is further evidence for Christianity in Britain as early as the 3rd century.

Appealing to – or thanking – a god might involve putting up a shrine, often at the roadside, carving a dedication on stone, or making a sacrifice – and the gods were expected to return the favour. Farmers and pregnant women made offerings to Serapis, the Egyptian god of fertility. People searching to cure an affliction appealed to Sulis Minerva, goddess of healing and cult deity at the bathing complex at Bath (Aquae Sulis), who was a combination of Celtic and Roman deities.

CHRISTIAN BRITAIN

A 4th-century mosaic floor picture from a villa at Hinton St Mary, Dorset, now at the British Museum. It may be the earliest-known face of Christ to be pictured in Britain.

CULTURE AND ART

ROMAN BRITISH ART mingled two traditions: Celtic and Roman. Celtic art was vigorously abstract, and the Romans (heavily influenced by the Greeks) introduced a more naturalistic representational style. Statues and busts were imported from the Mediterranean to decorate the villas and town houses of wealthy Romans in Britain, together with bronze, silver, glassware and pottery from Gaul. British artists copied these new styles, often matching them in quality – especially in metalwork (a Celtic tradition), pottery and local craft materials such as Yorkshire jet.

Roman artists produced work mostly to commission, having been asked to supply a painting, sculpture, mosaic or piece of jewellery by a wealthy citizen. The state, too, commissioned artists and architects for triumphal arches, columns, temples and other public buildings. Musicians were likewise hired out for a special occasion, though music – closely linked with poetry – was taught as part of the school curriculum and people with time on their hands might strum a lyre or think up a poem to recite to friends at parties.

Excavations have shown what Roman homes were like – and how they were decorated. Some town houses doubled as shops, with storerooms and workshops in small back rooms. Buildings were usually timber-framed, infilled with dried-mud bricks. Inside walls were plastered and painted with scenes or patterns to the owner's taste. Superior homes ran to decorated floors, produced by mosaic artists who laid down tiny tiles onto mortar. Less grand houses had walls of wattle (sticks) and daub (clay), with plain-coloured mosaic floors and again painted plaster walls.

Even big houses were sparsely furnished – tables, couches, folding stools, chests and caskets in the living room, wooden beds and cabinets in the bedroom. A portable

GODDESS OF LOVE

A bronze Venus, goddess of love and beauty, found at St Albans and probably from a household shrine or lararium, *where the family prayed each day, offering small gifts of wine or food.*

MOSAIC FLOOR

An elegant sea-shell mosaic from the 2nd century, now at the Verulamium Museum, St Albans.

PAINTED CEILING

A fine example of Roman interior decor, this painted ceiling with bird and flower design is from the Verulamium Museum, St Albans.

metal brazier, charcoal-fuelled, was lit for extra warmth on chilly evenings, and lighting after sunset came from small terracotta lamps filled with oil or candles.

Painted walls and mosaic floors have survived, often miraculously, to give us a glimpse of Roman interior design. Dark shades of red, green and brown were often chosen for walls, lightened by panels. Soothing pastoral scenes were popular subjects for decorated walls, and floors, along with mythology – Mediterranean and Celtic folklore and legend gave Roman artists a wealth of material to draw on. Carvings and statues filled niches in home and garden, as well as in public places. Stonemasons also earned a living from simple tombstone carvings for citizens and their wives.

Jewellers were always busy, for even poor Romans wore some kind of body decoration. A jeweller's shop was uncovered at St Albans, and evidence of silversmiths' workshops has been found in Silchester and Wroxeter. Some jewellers reproduced the abstract designs of Celtic art. Romans were especially fond of lucky charms, such as gorgons' heads, to thwart the evil eye, and they also liked small animal figures, such as bears and dogs.

THE ROMANS DEPART

ROMAN RULE IN BRITAIN expired as the Empire in the west withered and began to die. Rome's mighty Empire had grown too big to govern, except by rulers of rare talent – and such emperors were few. Weaker men lost their grip on the frontier territories and by AD 400 the Roman world had split into two empires: east and west – Constantinople and Rome. A showy brilliance dazzled in the Eastern Empire (later Byzantium), but the Western Empire was crumbling. Frontier provinces such as Britain, no longer jewels in the imperial crown, were threatened by ever-pressing 'barbarian' raiders.

Romans had a healthy respect for German barbarians and their fighting qualities. Proving constantly troublesome to them, the Romans had settled on containment, strengthening their frontiers to stop such tribes from crossing the Rhine. Britain provided some of the reinforcements, as front-line troops were withdrawn from this now settled and peaceful land for more pressing duties elsewhere. But without the legions, prosperous Britain tempted raiders who lurked just outside the Roman world. The island's people had to defend themselves, and did so in a way that proved ultimately fatal – by hiring mercenaries from the very people raiding their villas and farms.

The final blow fell in AD 410, when Rome's last troops left. Villas and towns came under renewed attack as waves of new invaders seized the land, driving the Britons westward. The towns, temples and immaculate villas of Roman Britain shrivelled into weed-covered ruins. The newcomers were farmers, not town-dwellers. They built their own wooden houses inside Roman walls, on Roman estates and alongside Roman roads, through which grass and weeds began to sprout. Britain once more lay beyond the boundaries of the Roman world.

WALLS FALL DOWN

Beside the Newgate in Chester are the remains of one of the 26 towers built around the Roman walls. Such a tower would have mounted a ballista, or huge crossbow, with a throwing range of over 400 metres (440 yards) – defences formidable enough to deter most aggressors, but not in the final reckoning to preserve Roman Britain.

DEFENDING A DYING ERA

Portchester Castle, Hampshire. Its eastern wall faces the seas which bore barbarian raiders to strike at Roman Britain. The present 12th-century castle was built inside the perimeter of the Roman fort, dating from the 3rd century and occupied until around AD 370.

FOR SPECIAL OCCASIONS

This bowl and lid comes from the Mildenhall treasure, a buried hoard unearthed in the 1940s. Dating from the 3rd to 4th centuries, it has a decorative frieze of animals and heads in profile, with a leaf pattern above. The magnificent piece would have been a family treasure.

FAREWELL TO ROMAN BRITAIN

ARTHUR'S STRONGHOLD?

Was Cadbury Castle hill fort in Somerset the stronghold of King Arthur? Re-fortified in the 6th century, the site included a hall building, designed for a great leader – perhaps the British warrior-king who defeated the Saxons.

LONG BEFORE THE ROMAN EMPIRE was split into east and west in AD 395, Britain had faced attack. The sea gave it no defence against seaborne invaders able to slip up rivers in shallow craft. Nor was the Roman navy equipped to chase off warriors by the boatload, crossing the Channel and North Sea with ease to raid temptingly rich targets along Britain's south coast. Not even a chain of coastal forts could defend the province against a sustained assault.

In AD 367, simultaneous attacks – by Scots from Ireland, Picts from Scotland and Saxons and Franks from across the North Sea – rocked Britain. Not enough Roman troops were left in the province to stop it from being overrun. The once-formidable British warriors – long forbidden to carry arms – could offer little defence against a year-long rampage of plunder, rape and murder. Roman Britain's 300-year-old foundations had begun to crack.

Of three generals sent from Rome to regain control over the ravaged province, the third – Theodosius – restored law and order, sent the raiders packing and brought in fresh troops. Though peace and some prosperity returned, these were doomed by political ambition. In AD 383 a power-hungry general, Magnus Maximus, seized control in Britain, leading the best troops out of the province to back his campaign as would-be emperor. He was defeated, but his actions cost Britain dear. The Western Empire was crumbling. When in AD 406 Gaul fell to an inrush of Germanic tribes surging across the Rhine, Britain was left virtually cut off from Rome. After the Roman army had pulled out – by AD 410 – Emperor Honorius released Britain from its allegiance, telling the Britons to defend themselves as best they could.

Desperate, British leaders hired German mercenaries to see off the menacing raiders, but these men soon turned on their paymasters. Land was there for the taking, and from the AD 440s onwards, invasion ships plunged westwards through the grey waters of the North Sea. Among those hiring Saxon soldiers, the monk-historian Gildas speaks of a 'proud tyrant' – named by *The Anglo-Saxon Chronicle* for AD 449 as Vortigern. His mercenaries are identified as Hengist and Horsa, who were given land in exchange for fighting the Picts. The result? The Saxons fought 'at first in aid of the Britons, but afterwards they fought against them.'

As more Angles, Saxons and Jutes moved in, there was last-ditch resistance. Gildas highlights a British victory, around AD 500, at Mons Badonicus (perhaps Badbury Rings in Dorset) won by the Roman-British leader identified in legend as King Arthur. It was a last rally. By the end of the AD 500s, the south belonged to the invaders. Some Britons stayed on; others, dispossessed, went west and into the hills of what is now Wales; yet others fled back across the sea, rather than endure slavery, and so founded Brittany.

Roman Britain had ended. A new country, England, was being shaped.

'The barbarians push us into the sea, the sea pushes us back to the barbarians.'

Welsh writer Gildas on the Britons' plight

LAST BASTION
The ten-sided Multangular Tower is almost all that remains of York's Roman walls. The row of Roman tiles nearly 2.4 metres (8 feet) above the ground can be seen below the upper medieval stonework.

PEVENSEY CASTLE

The Roman fort of Anderida was attacked by raiders from the sea in AD 491, almost a century after the legions had left Britain. Its defenders slaughtered, the site fell into ruin. William the Conqueror landed close by in 1066, whereupon Normans built a castle inside Roman walls.

THE FORTS OF THE SAXON SHORE

A Saxon copy of a Roman map showing Roman forts at Brancaster, Burgh, Walton, Bradwell, Reculver, Richborough, Dover, Lympne, Pevensey and Portchester.

IN THE HOPE OF DETERRING 'pirates', Roman strategy was to build a string of coastal forts, manned by lookout troops. These became known as the Forts of the Saxon Shore since many of the raiders they tried to repel were Saxons from the north German coastal plain.

The new forts were meant to shield south and east Britain as Hadrian's Wall protected the north. Their massive walls also substituted for a large garrison of experienced Roman troops that was no longer available. Reculver in north Kent, built in the 3rd century, signals that

'This year [AD 448] the Britons sent over the sea to Rome and begged for help against the Picts, but they had none ... And then they sent to the Angles.'

The Anglo-Saxon Chronicle

raiders from the sea were already then causing problems to Roman Britons. This fort is visible from far off, partly because a later twin-towered Saxon church stands ruined inside its defences.

〜

Twelve forts in all, from Norfolk in the east to Hampshire in the south, formed a defensive chain against invaders and raiders. At Richborough, where the Romans themselves had landed in AD 43, the walls were 8 metres (25 feet) high, of rubble and tile, faced with stone, and strengthened by towers and gateways. Further to the west stands Pevensey Castle, medieval-looking but in fact the site of a massive Roman fort, Anderida. Today's ruins lie 1.6 kilometres (1 mile) from the sea, but the Romans built its walls within earshot of the Channel's buffeting waves so that supplies could enter the fort by sea as well as by land. Pevensey's Roman walls enclose an area of 7.5 acres and, like Richborough's, they are massive – 4 metres (12 feet) thick and 8.5 metres (28 feet) high.

〜

Another 3rd-century fort – Portchester Castle – was sited on a strip of land jutting out into today's Portsmouth Harbour, to defend the estuary and port from raiders. The same site later proved useful to both Saxons and Normans, and the castle stands as an impressive monument to coastal defence down the ages. The Saxon shore forts proved reasonably

FORTS THAT FAILED

Burgh Castle, Norfolk, was among the Roman shore forts built to guard Britain from Saxon raids. But not even an east wall 200 metres (656 feet) long and 4.3 metres (14 feet) high could keep the raiders out.

effective – at least against mass attack – until AD 367, when a variety of invaders set upon Roman Britain from all sides. That year's horrors must have caused people to question the forts' value, though they were briefly recommissioned after a subsequent defence review. When the last Roman troops mustered for the last time and withdrew by AD 410, the forts remained – poignant symbols of a lost cause, and testament to the passing of the Britain that belonged to Rome.

THE ROMAN LEGACY

The Christian religion introduced by the Romans fragilely preserved the ancient world's learning in Britain after the Empire fell. Britons had been taught to read and write; they learned the stories and ideas of the Mediterranean world stemming from ancient Greece. Roman Britain had been merged into the wider sphere of Roman (Latin-using) culture. This legacy gave medieval Britain the basis for much of its law and literature, and so survives in the fabric of modern British life.

⤴

ROMAN AND CELTIC MIX

This beautifully enamelled bronze pan, decorated with Celtic motifs, was made in the 2nd century. It carries the name Aelius Draco, who was perhaps its owner, and lists four forts on Hadrian's Wall where he may have been stationed. The pan was found in the Staffordshire hills in 2003.

'Altogether they ruled in Britain four hundred and seventy years since Gaius Julius [Caesar] first sought the land.'

The Anglo-Saxon Chronicle, *entry for the year AD 409*

HEAD OF MEDUSA

Vivid detail from the mosaic floor of the heated changing room in the baths at Bignor Villa in Sussex. Only the grand-est Roman houses had such magnificent decoration.

TO HOMELY SAXON FARMERS, crumbling yet majestic Roman towns seemed the 'work of giants'. Later Arthurian legend-makers saw Roman Britain as a golden age, before a descent into 'Dark Age' chaos. In some respects little changed. Roman rule did not unite British tribes; indeed at first the Romans fostered division. Old tribal bonds and hostilities weakened as British nobles were Romanized, yet there was no real rupture in the familiar social order: land and wealth still determined social rank. Many Celtic traditions survived.

⤴

But the land was changed. Romans gave Britain a fine road system and its first canals. They began draining the Fens, creating a water-way system that still exists. Great tracts of land were put under cultivation, producing wheat as an important export. And – the greatest change of all – the Romans built around 50 large, walled towns, most of which evolved into thriving towns and cities of today.

Today, we prize fragments of buildings the Romans left – stretches of town walls, villas, forts, amphitheatres, baths. Archaeologists have dug their way into this lost world, unearthing everyday objects that may speak more vividly than stones or old manuscripts. Much still lies buried beneath fields, factories, high streets and roads – for future generations to discover.

INDEX

Adminius 7, 25

Agricola, Julius 56–7, 62, 63

Agrippina 35

amphitheatres 74, 75

amphorae 64, 66, 67

Anglesey 11, 44–5, 46–7

Anglo-Saxon Chronicle, The 91, 93, 94

Antonine Itinerary 41

Antonine Wall 57

Aquae Sulis *see* Bath

aquilifers 44

armour 13, 29, 53, 54–5

army *see* legions and legionaries; soldiers, Roman

art 15, 70, 86–7; *see also* mosaics

Arthur, King 90, 91, 94

Atrebates 17, 26, 29, 37

Augustus, Emperor 65

auxiliary troops 54–5

Badbury Rings 91

Baginton 50

ballistas 34, 89; *see also* weaponry

barbarian invasions 89–93

Bath 40, 60–1, 77, 85

bathhouses 33, 61, 68, 69, 74, 76–7

'Battersea' shield 21

battles 13, 14, 17, 20–7, 37–9, 43, 47, 56–7

Belgae 16, 17, 31

Bignor Villa 69, 94

Boudicca 37, 48–51, 61, 66

Brigantes 13, 16, 17, 38–9, 43, 44, 45, 51, 56

Burgh Castle 93

burials 9, 15, 16, 39

Butser Ancient Farm 8

Cadbury Castle 90

Caerleon 32, 41, 56, 74, 76

Caerwent 56

Caesar, Julius 5, 7, 16, 19, 22–5, 38

Caledonia 51, 53, 56–7

Calgacus 56

Caligula 25, 26

Camulodunum 10, 12, 13, 24, 25, 27, 30, 48, 72

Canterbury 75

Caratacus 7, 27, 28–9, 37, 39, 42–3, 53

Cartimandua 29, 43, 44

Cassivellaunus 7, 24–5

Castell Dinas Bran 28

Castell Henlys 11

Catus, Decianus 51

Catuvellauni 7, 13, 16, 17, 24–5, 26, 28–9, 31, 38

Celtic art 86–7

Celtic traditions and beliefs 15, 21, 84, 94; *see also* Druids

Celtic tribes 7, 14–15, 16–17, 24–5, 38–9

Celts 5–21 *passim*, 25–6, 46, 56–7, 61, 76

centurions 54, 55

chariots, use of 20, 21, 22, 24, 26, 39, 61, 74

Chedworth Villa 69, 84

Chester 40, 56, 64, 74, 89

Chesterholm 59, 82; *see also* Vindolanda

Chesters Roman Fort 52

Chichester 29

children 15, 80–1

Christianity 85, 94

Cicero 7

Cirencester 5, 79, 81

citizenship, Roman 63

Classicianus, Julius 51, 62, 66

Claudius, Emperor 19, 26–7, 28, 29, 30, 35, 43, 48, 49

Cogidubnus 29, 53, 70

coins, finds of 16, 48, 56, 65

Colchester 10, 33, 49, 61, 72, 75; *see also* Camulodunum

coloniae 33, 48, 62, 72

Constantine, Emperor 37, 85

Constantinople 89

cremation 15

Cunobelinus 7, 24, 25, 26, 42

curse tablets 77, 84

Cytiau'r Gwyddelod 11

Deceangli 16, 17, 39

Didius Gallus, Aulus 44, 63

Din Lligwy 44

Dio Cassius 26

Dobunni 16, 17, 29

Dover lighthouse 36–7

dress 53, 78, 80

Druids and Druidism 44–7

Dumnonii 16, 17, 34

Durotriges 13, 16, 17, 31, 34

'The Dying Gaul' 7

education 81, 86

emperor-worship 85

Empire, Roman, map of 5

entertainments 74–5, 81; *see also* games

Epona 15, 47

Ermine Street 19, 40, 41

family life 80–1

farming 8–9, 68–9, 89

fashions 78

festivals 74, 84

Fishbourne Palace 29, 53, 69, 70–1

food 78-9, 80, 81

fortresses and forts 18–19, 30–3, 39–40, 50, 52–3, 54, 58, 59, 82–3, 92–3; *see also* hill forts

forum 61, 72, 73

Fosse Way 19, 34, 40

Frontinus, Julius 56, 63

funerals 81; *see also* burials

furniture 11, 86

gambling 74, 77

games 14, 59, 74, 81; *see also* entertainment

gardens 71, 81, 87

Gaul 5, 10, 15, 16, 19, 21, 61, 64, 67, 86, 91

Gibbon, Edward 5, 61

gladiators 74–5

Gloucester 34, 72

gods and goddesses 13, 15, 34, 46, 47, 53, 74, 77, 84–5, 86

government and governors of Britain 62–3, 66–7, 70, 75

grave goods 9, 14–15, 16

Gundestrup Cauldron 46

Hadrian, Emperor 52, 57, 58

Hadrian's Wall 4–5, 19, 37, 47, 52–3, 57, 58–9, 83, 92

Hengist and Horsa 91

hill forts 10, 12–13, 28, 34, 56, 57, 90; *see also* Maiden Castle

Hinton St Mary Villa 85

Hod Hill 34–5

Honorius, Emperor 91

Horkstow Villa 61

houses 10–11, 64, 78–9, 80–1, 86–7; *see also* villas

Housesteads 59
hypocausts 69, 71

Iceni 16, 17, 29, 35, 38–9, 48,
    50–1, 61

jewellery 16, 78, 79, 87
Julianus, Emperor 79

Latin language 62, 82
law 62, 72, 94
legions and legionaries 22,
    23, 26, 28, 30–1, 33, 42–3,
    44, 54–5, 56, 59, 85
leisure 74–5
Lincoln 30, 31, 40, 72
Lindow Man 47
Londinium *see* London
London 25, 48–9, 62, 64–7,
    72, 73
Lullingstone Villa 61, 85
Lunts, The 50

magistrates 62, 63, 72
Maiden Castle 6–7, 10, 13,
    19, 34
marriage 15, 80–1
Maximus, Magnus 91
medical treatment 54
mercenaries, use of 89, 91
Mildenhall treasure 89
milestones 41
mining 64
Mithras 53, 85
money 65; *see also* coins
Mons Badonicus 91
Mons Graupius 56
mosaics 5, 70–1, 61, 69, 73,
    85, 86–7, 94
music 81, 86

Nemesis 74

Nero, Emperor 44

Ordovices 16, 17, 28, 39
Ostorius Scapula, Publius
    35, 37, 38–9, 43, 44, 63

Paulinus, Gaius Suetonius
    44, 48, 50, 51, 63
Pen-y-Gaer 9, 13
Petillius Cerialis, Quintus 56
Pevensey Castle 92, 93
Picts 56, 90, 91, 93
Piercebridge 68
Plautius, Aulus 26, 27, 30,
    34–5, 37, 63
Pliny 46
Portchester Castle 88–9, 93
pottery 64, 67, 79, 86, 94
Prasutagus 29, 48
Puffin Island 46–7
Pytheas 8

Reculver 92–3
religion 46–7, 84–5; *see also*
    gods and goddesses
Richborough 18–19, 40, 92,
    93
roads 19, 40–1, 53, 54, 61,
    64, 89, 94
Roman Empire, map of 5
Romanization 53, 61, 64,
    68, 80, 94

sacrifice 46, 47, 85
St Alban 85
St Albans 49, 74–5, 78, 85,
    86–7
Samian ware 64, 79
Saxon Shore, Forts of the
    92–3
seasonal festivals 84
Serapis 85

shrines 71, 74, 85, 86
Silchester 30, 37, 63, 87
Silures 16, 17, 28, 39, 44, 49,
    56
slaves 14, 78–9, 80
Snettisham hoard 25
soldiers, Roman 31, 54–5,
    58, 85; *see also* legions
    and legionaries
Sparsholt 69
Spettisbury Rings 34
Stanegate Road 58, 82–3
Stanwick 13, 56
statues 86–7
Strabo 20
Suetonius 27, 31
Sulis Minerva 77, 85

tablets *see* curse tablets;
    Vindolanda; writing
    tablets
Tacitus 9, 19, 20, 28, 29, 37,
    39, 42, 43, 44, 45, 48, 49,
    50, 53, 56, 57, 61, 62
Tammonus, Saenius 63
taxation 48, 51, 62, 72
temples 48, 49, 71, 77, 84
testudo formation 43, 55
Thames, River 21, 24, 25,
    26, 49, 65–6
theatres 75; *see also*
    amphitheatres
Togodumnus 7, 26
tombstones 31, 33, 38–9, 53,
    62, 65, 66, 81, 82, 87
torcs 25
towns and town life 10–11,
    19, 30, 33, 37, 61, 64, 68,
    72–3, 89, 94
trade 8, 64–7
Trajan's Column 22–3, 29,
    33, 42

Traprain Law 57
Tre'r Ceiri 12
tribes of Britain 7, 14–15,
    16–17, 24–5, 38–9
Trinovantes 12, 13, 16, 17,
    25, 48, 72

Vegetius 43
Vellocatus 44
Veneti 16
Venutius 44, 56
Veranius, Quintus 44
Vercingetorix 16
Verica 26
Verulamium *see* St Albans
Vespasian 31, 34
villas 19, 61, 68–9, 85, 86,
    89, 94; *see also*
    Fishbourne Palace
Vindolanda 58, 59, 64,
    82–3
Virgil 68, 83
Vortigern 91
Votadini 17, 57

Walbrook stream 51, 66
wall paintings 69, 71, 85,
    86, 87
Watling Street 19, 40
weaponry 20–1, 25, 27,
    28–9, 34, 38, 39, 54, 55
Wheeldale 40
White Horse, Uffington 13
William the Conqueror 92
Winchester 69, 73
wines 64, 67, 79
writing tablets 82–3
Wroxeter 31, 40, 56, 73, 74,
    76, 87

York 30, 31, 32, 37, 64, 72,
    78, 91